THE MONEY COACH

Your game plan for Growth, Tax Relief and Security

THE MONEY COACH

Riley Moynes

Your game plan for Growth, Tax Relief and Security

Copp Clark Longman Ltd.

ASHLAR HOUSE INC.

Published by Copp Clark Longman and Ashlar House Publishing &
Promotions

ISBN 0-7730-5360-3

Canadian Cataloguing in Publication Data

Moynes, Riley E., 1944-
The money coach: your game plan for growth, security and tax relief

2nd ed.
ISBN 0-7730-5360-3

1. Finance, Personal - Canada I.Title.

HG179.M69 1993 332.024'01'0971 C93-095158-1

Design & Art Direction: Smart Work
Illustration & Computer Graphics: Kyle Gell, Stephen MacEachern,
                                            Allan Moon
Cover Design: Overdrive
Printing and Binding: Quebecor Printing

Acknowledgements

Many individuals and organizations have contributed their time,
support and expertise in the development of this project. Sincere thanks
are extended to Jim Fraser, Lee Daugharty, Cathy Holyoke, Peter
Matthews, Sabine Steinbrecher, Tom Ryan, Peggy Adamson, Alan
Strathdee, Albert Fong, Donna Brown, Allan Moon, Jeff Miller, Les
Petriw, The Fraser Institute, Mackenzie Financial Corporation, Canadian
Institute of Actuaries, The Equion Group, Home Earnings Reverse
Mortgage Corporation and the Investment Funds Institute of Canada.
I wish to particularly thank my wife Yvonne for her ongoing support
and eternal patience; she continues to be the "wind beneath my wings."

Printed and bound in Canada

1 2 3 4 5   5360-3   97 96 95 94 93

TABLE OF CONTENTS

THE
GAME
PLAN

Get GROWING

GOAL 1

CHOP TAXES

BUILD YOUR DEFENCE

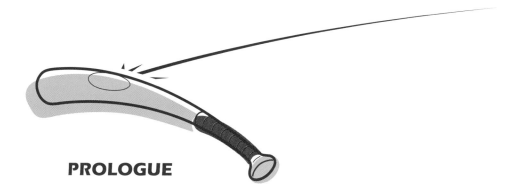

PROLOGUE

Several years ago when I left the field of public education, my practical education began.

True, I had acquired a great deal of formal education. I graduated from elementary school, from high school, and from university. Then I returned to earn both Masters and Doctoral degrees. I had spent 20 years as a teacher at the elementary, secondary, and university levels. I had coached football, basketball, and hockey teams with some success. I had worked as an educational administrator, serving as both a Superintendent of Schools and a Director of Education. I had most definitely benefited from, and perhaps even contributed to, the educational system. And I had some experience with winning. But my practical education was sadly lacking.

About 10 years ago I began to have a nagging feeling — one that became more pronounced every year — that I was so busy taking care of my job responsibilities that I was neglecting not only my family but also my finances. My salary

kept getting bigger (along with my tax bill), but it didn't seem that we were making much financial progress, and I certainly didn't feel as if I was winning the money game we are all forced to play. Worse still, I came to realize that I didn't even know how to change the situation.

To be sure, I was largely responsible for this vast financial ignorance. But I also realized that to a large degree, I was financially ignorant because I had never been taught some of the financial basics.

Here I was, a competent, experienced professional with many academic and professional qualifications, almost completely lacking in knowledge about such basics as how to select the best mortgage, how to plan for my children's university education, how to reduce my tax liability legitimately, and how to prepare for a secure and carefree retirement. And as I began to discuss the topic with colleagues and friends, I found that they were in basically the same boat!

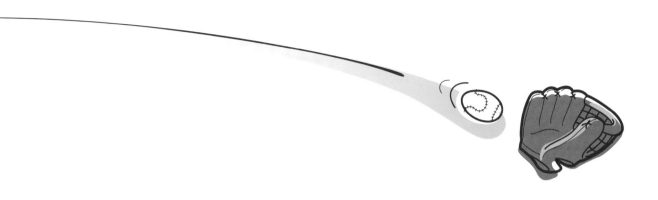

I therefore decided to master the secret mysteries of acquiring wealth — assuming that it would be a long and painful process. To my absolute surprise, I discovered that in finance as in many other fields, the great truths are the simplest. I learned the basics in a comparatively short time and came to realize that they are essentially straightforward commonsense principles.

And then I got angry! It struck me that if I had learned these fundamentals 20 years earlier, and applied them, I would have been much further ahead financially than I was at the time. I was also angry because I recognized that the only thing standing between people and the achievement of their fondest financial dreams are two simple obstacles. One is the basic knowledge of what to do and how to do it. The second is a decision to act.

The result of this was that in the space of a very short period of time I saw an opportunity. It was an opportunity to become a coach and teacher again (as opposed to an administrator), and to provide a much needed educational service to the growing number of people who are coming to realize that their future financial security must be taken into their hands — not left exclusively to a pension plan. And certainly not left to the government which is quickly displaying in stark terms that it cannot manage its own finances, let alone yours or mine.

This book has been written to share with you the simple, commonsense ideas and principles that if acted upon will, over a period of time, create the assets that can help ensure the secure, worry-free retirement years we all dream of — but that very few of us achieve.

Read on, learn, enjoy, and act! You'll be glad you did.

Riley E. Moynes

INTRODUCTION

Are you winning the money "game"?

Do you know that you're **playing** the money game?

Like it or not, we are all **forced** to play this game from the time we begin to earn money through the rest of our lives. Taxes must be paid, bills must be paid, and loans must be paid. Money must be allocated for food, rent or mortgage, telephone, car payments, credit cards, insurance, new clothes for the kids, etc. Savings are necessary for that trip, for schooling, for retirement. The list seems endless.

How do you learn to play the money game successfully? The sad truth is that some people **never** do. Those who succeed often do so in a hit or miss fashion, more through good luck than good management. Some of us learn from parents or others, although most of what they learned was through sometimes bitter experience.

Unfortunately, very little formal attention is given to the topic in our schools. The attitude seems to be that it's either something that comes naturally (like walking and talking), or that it's not all that important. Both assumptions are very, very wrong!

Sometimes we turn to "professionals" for help, and they can be helpful in certain ways. Accountants have detailed knowledge of the Income Tax Act, and while that is important to the rules of the financial game, it's by no means the only part. Lawyers who specialize in tax law can be helpful in certain areas, but beyond that may have no particular financial expertise. A bank manager may be helpful when it comes to providing a needed mortgage or loan, or in telling you what the current GIC or savings account rates are, but there's a lot more to the game than that.

Then there's Revenue Canada. Again, someone there **may** be able to help you, although I've been given four different answers to the same tax-related question by four different RevCan employees!

And again, their expertise is limited to aspects and interpretations of the Income Tax Act. Even so, Revenue Canada is the ultimate **referee** in the money game.

So to whom do you turn to help you play the game effectively and successfully? You need a money coach. That's why this book was written: to help you understand the financial "big picture," and to help you develop the skills and knowledge necessary in order to compete successfully in the financial game. You're forced to play the game, so you might as well get all the help you can to play it well!

But good coaching does not come exclusively from a book. After you read this one, I urge you to find your own money coach who will continue to

work with you. An effective coach will keep you up to date on the continual changes to the rules of the game. Your money coach will help you to further develop the financial skills you'll learn from this book by practising them with you and giving feedback on how well you're using them.

Some people call them financial advisers or planners, investment consultants, insurance agents, or stock brokers. I call them "money coaches." I urge you to find one with whom you're comfortable, in whom you have confidence, and who provides you with outstanding service. It can be a very satisfying, productive, and successful relationship as well as a positive learning experience.

And good luck as you play the financial game. I am confident that *The Money Coach* will help you play it successfully. You may even turn out to be a star in the game!

THE GAME PLAN

I t's not how much money you make that's important, it's how much you keep.

Quite simply, this book is about accumulating wealth so that you can become "financially free." To me, you are financially free when you can do what you want, where you want, when you want, and with whom you want. To some, that will enable travel and the acquisition of things; for others, it will enable charitable donations and assistance to family and friends.

Unfortunately, three major obstacles prevent us from keeping as much as we'd like — and as much as we deserve.

These three obstacles are:

- **taxes**
- **inflation**
- **no plan**

TAXES

In theory, taxes are imposed by governments at all levels and paid by Canadians in order to fund services that are required or desired by the people. These include such diverse services as national defence, transportation, highway construction, mail delivery, garbage pick up, and many others.

Unfortunately, for a variety of reasons including government mismanagement, Canadians are now among the most heavily taxed people in the world. One research group, The Fraser Institute in Vancouver, calculates that while in 1961 only 34% of the income of the average Canadian home was paid in taxes of all kinds, the figure had increased to 44% in 1993.

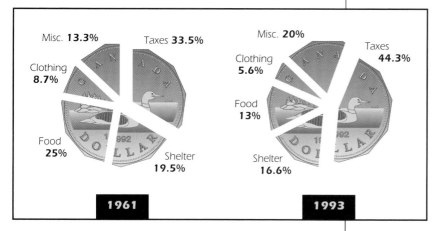

	Misc. **13.3%**	Taxes **33.5%**
Clothing **8.7%**		
Food **25%**		Shelter **19.5%**

1961

	Misc. **20%**	Taxes **44.3%**
Clothing **5.6%**		
Food **13%**		Shelter **16.6%**

1993

The trend appears to be inevitable: an ever increasing amount of personal income consumed by taxes.

Unfortunately, most Canadians seem to be resigned to this sorry situation. You'll learn by reading on, however, that there are several ways of reducing your tax burden and keeping more of your own money.

Think of paying taxes as a game. You probably wouldn't decide to play a game before you knew the rules — you'd be afraid of embarrassing yourself publicly, and you know that you can't play any game effectively without knowing the rules that apply. Your coach or someone teach-

es you the rules, and you can then play more effectively.

It's the same with taxes except that we are all forced to play the tax game — we have no choice. All the rules apply, but we don't know them well. Therefore, we play the tax game poorly. And when was the last time your friendly Revenue Canada representative called to suggest tax reduction strategies or to clarify the tax rules for you? Revenue Canada is not the coach — it's the umpire. You must either get a money coach (a financial adviser, a tax lawyer, an accountant, a trusted friend) or teach yourself. Most of us do neither. Small wonder we don't play the tax game well and therefore, pay more in taxes than is necessary!

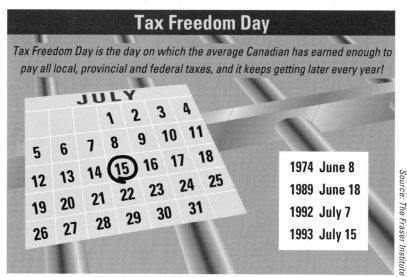

Tax Freedom Day

Tax Freedom Day is the day on which the average Canadian has earned enough to pay all local, provincial and federal taxes, and it keeps getting later every year!

JULY

			1	2	3	4
5	6	7	8	9	10	11
12	13	14	(15)	16	17	18
19	20	21	22	23	24	25
26	27	28	29	30	31	

1974	June 8
1989	June 18
1992	July 7
1993	July 15

Source: The Fraser Institute

This date includes government deficits, since at some point taxes will have to be higher by the amount of the deficit. Tax freedom day, excluding deficits, was June 15, 1993

INFLATION

While most people seem to be aware of taxes (though they may not know what to do about them), they seem to be unaware of the insidiousness of inflation. It truly is a silent, stalking enemy that assaults — and can even destroy — our financial health in the same way that cancer attacks and can ruin our physical health.

In simple terms, inflation eats into and reduces our buying power on an ongoing basis. Twenty years ago in 1973 it cost 6¢ to mail a first class letter in Canada; in 1993 it cost 46¢ (43 + 3 GST)! That's inflation! If this rate of inflation continues for the next twenty years, it will cost $2.64 to mail a first class letter.

Inflation also devastates your investment returns. Over the last decade, inflation has virtually swallowed up or offset most wage increases that have been achieved by Canadians.

The result — most people are "treading water" at best, and not getting ahead in real terms.

Inflation also hits hard at pensioners who do not have inflation protection as part of their plan. It cuts the purchasing power of a $40,000 pension in half to $20,000 in about 12 years (at an average inflation rate of 6%).

Always take inflation into account when calculating investment gains. It's the only way to get a true sense of the progress that has been achieved.

◆ ◆ ◆

On the bright side, there is one good thing that can be said of inflation: It has allowed virtually every Canadian homeowner to live in a more expensive neighbourhood without moving.

INFLATION'S BITE

NOMINAL vs. REAL RATES OF RETURN
50 YEARS (1943-1992)

■ **Nominal return**

■ **Real return**
(nominal return minus inflation)
Inflation = 4.6%

	COMMON SHARES	GOVERNMENT BONDS	91–DAY T–BILLS

(y-axis: 12%, 10%, 8%, 6%, 4%, 2%, 0)

Source: Harry H. Panjer and Keith P. Sharp, "Report on Canadian Economic Statistics, 1924–1992," Canadian Institute of Actuaries, May 1993.

NO PLAN

If you don't know where you are going, any road will do.

— *Chinese proverb*

Unfortunately, this quotation is true for the vast majority of Canadians. Over 90% of us do nothing that could reasonably be called financial planning.

It's not that people plan to fail. Rather, they fail to plan.

Financial planning is essentially the proper handling of income and cash to meet your goals. A financial plan should be "one page simple" and generally should not include a monthly or weekly budget. I don't know anyone who became wealthy by budgeting; not only are those who try it usually unsuccessful, but they also tend to be boring conversationalists. Concentrate instead on the "big picture."

So far we have outlined the situation that many people find themselves in.

- They're paying large amounts in tax; likely more than necessary.
- They're being hurt by inflation without even realizing it.
- They don't know what they're trying to achieve and have no plan to achieve it.

Now let's look at what can and should be.

COACH'S PLAYBOOK

How to build a financial plan

A financial plan should contain three simple parts:

Part 1. A snapshot of where you are financially, i.e., a statement of assets, obligations, and income.

Part 2. A statement or at least a sense of where you want to be in the short term (one year) and the longer term (three to five years), i.e., a goal or goals.

Part 3. A list of actions to be taken to get you from where you are to where you want to be.

Most people have no difficulty with Parts 1 or 2 of their financial plan; Part 3 can be more difficult unless you know some of the strategies. That's what this book will help you to learn. But you should also have some help from someone you trust in putting together a series of actions to be taken or decisions to be made; in other words, find yourself a money coach.

Ideally you won't depend too much on others to help you develop and implement your plan. Ultimately, we must all take responsibility for our own financial future. Fortunately, the basic principles to help you do that are really very simple. Not only can you learn them but you can also learn to apply them. That's where the fun and the results come!

PART 1

General information

YES   NO

◇   ◇   1. Do you have a current will?

◇   ◇   2. Do you have a child/grandchild education fund?

◇   ◇   3. Do you anticipate a significant inheritance?

◇   ◇   4. Do you face any major life changes (marriage, job, move)?

◇   ◇   5. Is your home registered jointly with your spouse?

6. What is your current income from all sources?

_____

7. What is the approximate rate of return on your current RRSP?

_____

8. How much life insurance coverage do you have?

_____

9. How much income tax did you pay last year?

_____

10. How many years to expected retirement?

_____

11. Expected retirement income?

_____

Current net worth

Assets		Obligations	
Savings	_____	Mortgage PIT	_____
Stocks, bonds, mutual funds	_____	Credit cards	_____
Home	_____	Loans	_____
Other property	_____	Support payment	_____
Autos	_____	Line of credit	_____
RRSP's	_____	Other mortgages	_____
Other	_____	Other	_____
Total assets	_____	Total obligations	_____

Net worth (assets-obligations) _____

Assessment

What aspects of your current situation are you:
Most pleased about?

_____

_____

_____

Least pleased about?

_____

_____

_____

PART 2

What are your current financial priorities? (e.g. buy new car, pay off mortgage, pay less tax, save for vacation, renovate, etc.)

_____

_____

_____

Where do you want to be financially in 5 to 10 years? (e.g. have no mortgage, pay less tax, acquire an investment portfolio, prepare for retirement, start your own business.)

_____

_____

_____

THE 3 GOALS OF FINANCIAL INDEPENDENCE

I'm convinced that if people patiently and consistently focus on the following simple financial goals, they would be well on the road to financial independence.

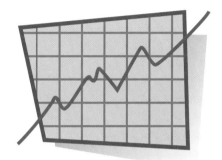

Δ growth

Δ tax relief

Δ security

These goals will represent different priorities for different people depending on their age and circumstances. But taken together, they represent a very powerful set of objectives.

We can achieve all three key objectives. But to do so, we must be prepared to make some decisions that do not always have "guaranteed" results. I'm convinced this is the preferred way to go.

············ *COACH'S QUOTE* ············

"Remember, you'll never get rich by putting all your money in the bank."

These few pages have attempted to set the stage for later chapters and to put the more specific suggestions that follow in perspective.

We have identified your financial goals of growth, tax relief, and security. You know, at least in general terms, where you want to go . You're ready to examine the strategies and suggestions that lie ahead. You're ready to put your game plan into effect.

Get *GROWING*

A strong commitment to seek growth is vital for two main reasons:

1. To avoid being limited exclusively to pension income in retirement

Some Canadians are fortunate because they belong to a pension plan where they work. But even the best of these plans will provide only up to a maximum of 70% of your pre-retirement income in retirement. Many Canadians will live in retirement on as little as 25% of their former income, and that prospect is scary.

Fewer than one half of all Canadians are enrolled in a Registered Retirement Savings Plan (RRSP) or company pension plan, and one third have no savings or investment program for retirement.

At most, benefits from the Canada Pension Plan and Old Age Security replace only about one quarter of your earnings. The maximum currently available from all government sources is a little more than $1,000 per month, and there are growing concerns about the future viability of the government's retirement security system as our population continues to age and fewer younger people contribute to it.

INCOME GAP AT RETIREMENT

$50,000 —	
$40,000 —	
$30,000 —	
$20,000 —	
$10,000 —	
0 —	
Pre-Retirement Income	Canada Pension Plan & Old Age Security after retirement

Contributions to CPP are projected to rise substantially over the next several decades, and if future generations of voters ultimately reject higher contributions as politically unacceptable, governments will be forced to dramatically reduce the plan's payouts. As a result, Canadians will have to fall back more and more on their own resources in retirement.

Some people seem to think that's okay, and they'll simply adjust their retirement lifestyle accordingly. I say you shouldn't be prepared to accept anything less in retirement than the income you enjoyed in your peak earning years!

After all, you'll have more time available (about one quarter to one third of your life). You've spent your whole life working and often putting off doing things you really wanted to do, like travelling. In retirement you'll have the time, but will you have the money?

Probably not if you don't do something to supplement your income. For most people, that means achieving growth in their investments before retirement. We'll offer specific suggestions how starting on Page 21.

Then there are those who don't have a pension at all. It's absolutely vital that these folks put money away now so they'll have a decent income

when they retire and not be reliant on government cheques for support.

Your goal should be to achieve the same level of income in retirement as you enjoyed in your peak earning years.

2. To beat inflation and taxes by the widest margin possible

As we noted in the previous chapter, inflation and taxes are two major adversaries as we try to get ahead financially.

Your real rate of return is what you make after taxes and inflation.

It is generally agreed that a 3% real rate of return is pretty good; of course, the higher the better.

The problem is that many people are simply treading water.

If you put your money in a savings account or buy term deposits, Canada Savings Bonds, or Guaranteed Investment Certificates (GICs), you're probably not getting ahead financially.

Here's why:

1992 Canada Savings Bonds

Advertised Rate of Return	6.0%
Taxes (at 50%)	− 3.0%
Inflation (current)	− 2.0%
Real Rate of Return	= 1.0%

So, if seeking significant growth is your objective (as it should be), you will usually not achieve it by putting your money in the bank or by buying CSBs or GICs.

Wouldn't you rather experience this?

Rate of return	16.0%
Taxes (at 50%)	− 8.0%
Inflation (current)	− 2.0%
Real Rate of Return	= 6.0%

Now you're making progress. You achieved 16.0% return on investment, rather than settling for 6.0%, and your real rate of return is above that magic 3.0% level. It's a gain of 6.0% rather than 1.0%.

And it's easy to do. Begin building your strategy using the following steps to achieve growth.

- ☐ Start now!
- ☐ Pay yourself first!
- ☐ Be consistent!
- ☐ Be an "owner," not a "loaner"!
- ☐ Put your money to work in mutual funds!

1. START NOW!

Why start now? It's important to start now because time is a critical element in achieving growth; the earlier the better and better late then never.

Let's assume you set a goal to have $100,000 at age 65 to supplement your other sources of income at that time. Believe it or not, if you are 25 now, you can achieve this goal by saving only $10.22 per month (at 12%). Most people can find $10.22 a month if they want to, especially if they know what it will turn into at age 65.

But if you're 55 now and want to achieve the same goal — $100,000 at age 65 — you're going to have to put aside $446.36 per month (at 12%) — 43 times more than you would have had to save monthly at age 25!

So it's easy to see that if you want to be financially independent, you must start now. The longer you wait, the more it will cost you to achieve your goal, as shown below.

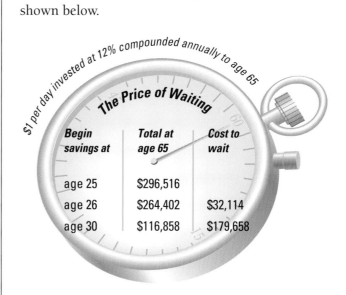

$1 per day invested at 12% compounded annually to age 65

The Price of Waiting

Begin savings at	Total at age 65	Cost to wait
age 25	$296,516	
age 26	$264,402	$32,114
age 30	$116,858	$179,658

By waiting five years before starting to invest (from age 25 to 30), it actually costs you $179,658!

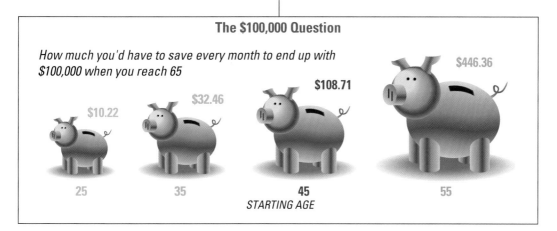

The $100,000 Question

How much you'd have to save every month to end up with $100,000 when you reach 65

$10.22	$32.46	$108.71	$446.36
25	35	45	55

STARTING AGE

Money Coach Rule

Start now to ensure that you're part of the minority of Canadians who retire with financial dignity.

2. PAY YOURSELF FIRST: USE THE 10% SOLUTION!

At the first of each month, before you pay a single bill, write yourself a cheque for at least 10% of your income and make it part of your regular investment program.

Who deserves it more than you do? After all, you earned it.

Why is it so vital to pay yourself first?

The discouraging truth is that according to Statistics Canada, a full 43% of those over 65 must now rely on the Guaranteed Income Supplement to see them through their retirement years. They live at subsistence levels, and as can be seen from the charts below, the situation is substantially worse for women.

Many are also relying on Canada Pension Plan (CPP) benefits to assist them in their old age. First of all, these benefits will not enable most people to live at the level they did during their working career and secondly, as the accompanying information shows, there are fewer and fewer people contributing to CPP in relation to the number drawing from it as time goes on and as the population ages.

It is quite possible that when you retire, CPP will not provide much of anything for your retirement. Canada will experience a dramatic increase in the number of seniors in the future. As a result there is no guarantee that social programs once considered universal will be continued. There is no contract with the government; programs can be wiped out.

Who'll be wealthy

For 100 men or women starting their career at age 25, the following situation will exist at age 65.

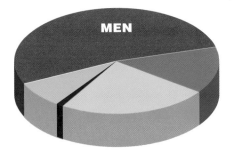

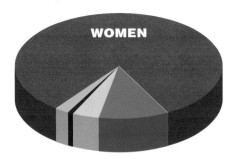

- 53 men, 82 women will require financial assistance from family, friends and/or the government

- 14 men, 11 women will be working whether they wanted to or not

- 8 men, 2 women will be financially secure enjoying a lifestyle close to what they were used to when they worked

- 24 men, 4 women will be dead

- 1 man, 1 woman will be wealthy

Source: Statistics Canada, 1991

Even if you contribute to a pension plan at work (and only about 40% of Canadians do), your pension income will generally not provide you with more then 60% to 70% of your peak earning income. If you don't contribute to a pension plan, government assistance will provide only about 25% of your earnings in your peak earning years. The maximum one can currently receive from both Canada and provincial government plans is a little over $12,000 per year; most receive less. And what you do receive is taxed!

Remember the goal: to retire at an income level the same as you achieved during your peak earning years. It is unwise to rely on someone else to provide for your financial future. No one cares about your future the way you do.

Start now to supplement your pension income or to create your own pension through an investment program consisting of at least 10% of your earnings. Pay yourself first!

◆ ◆ ◆

THE RULE OF 72

Want to know how long it will take to double your money? Just divide 72 by your investment rate of return. For example, if a mutual fund you're investing in produces an average annual compound rate of return of 12%, you will double your money in 72÷12=6 years.

Rate of Return	Time Required to Double Investment
4%	18 years
5%	14.4 years
6%	12 years
7%	10.3 years
8%	9 years
9%	8 years
10%	7.2 years
11%	6.5 years
12%	6 years

3. BE CONSISTENT!

Time, as we have just seen, is one key element in achieving growth.

The other significant part of the equation is consistency — but it doesn't take much money to get started, and a little will turn into a lot.

The following chart (The Power of Compounding, next page) illustrates how it works. Let's assume you can invest only $120 per month over a long term and that you can obtain a 17.9% return on your money. In 25 years it'll grow to more than $524,000; in 35 years, to more than $2.7 million. And in 40 years, you'll have more than $6.2 million!

I don't know what the Seven Wonders of the World are, but I know what the Eighth Wonder is: compounding

Baron Rothschild

It sounds unbelievable, but it's true. Time and consistency are powerful! Your $120 per month (about only $28 per week) turns into $6.2 million after 40 years.

The growth of money over time is called "compounding." And it's one of the most amazing and exciting financial concepts of all.

Many people don't think a few extra percentage points of return amount to much money. They are wrong.

Just a few percentage points of return compounded over several years can make a difference of thousands and thousands of additional dollars. Here's how it works.

The accompanying chart (Long–term Returns) shows what happens when you invest $3,500 each year for 30 years at different rates.

It's clear that the rate of return has a huge impact on the final amount of money available and reinforces the fact that we should always seek out these few extra percentage points of return, in order to achieve the greatest growth possible.

Long – Term Returns
How a $3,500 annual investment grows over 30 years

Value of Investment

Rate of Return	10%	11%	12%	13%	14%
	$633,302	$773,196	$946,024	$1,159,603	$1,423,580

Note that a difference of only 1% (from 10% to 11%) produces an added return of about $140,000.

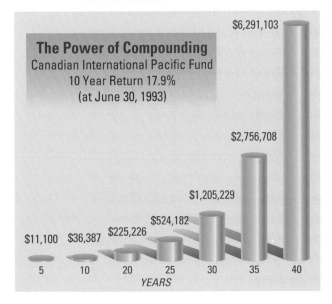

The Power of Compounding
Canadian International Pacific Fund
10 Year Return 17.9%
(at June 30, 1993)

YEARS	5	10	20	25	30	35	40
	$11,100	$36,387	$225,226	$524,182	$1,205,229	$2,756,708	$6,291,103

Pay Yourself 10% First + Start Early + Magic of Compounding = Financial Independence

COACH'S PLAYBOOK

Pay off your bank loans and credit cards

It's true that debt — a bank loan or a mortgage — can help to focus your attention and ensure that the payments are made. It's a form of "forced savings." Many of us won't save $100 a month but will pay back a loan at $100 a month. The effect is similar. However, there is a major difference. When you have a loan, you're paying interest on that loan! That means it's costing you money — and it's after-tax dollars.

And that is particularly true of credit cards. Several major Canadian credit cards charge in the range of 15% to 18% and some have been higher than that. Yet, thousands of people continue to hold CSBs or GICs, which are fully taxable, at the same time that they have outstanding consumer loans. No! No! No!

One more thought. If you've got more than one loan, first pay off the one that's costing you the most. If you've got a loan at 10% and one at 8%, pay off or at least reduce the 10% loan first.

Alternatively, consider consolidating two or more outstanding loans; you may be able to negotiate a lower rate than you're paying now and you may be able to reduce your monthly payments at the same time. In short, get rid of your non-deductible debt as soon as you can. It'll make you feel great, and it's one of the best moves you can make!

Money Coach Rule

The message should be clear: pay off car loans, furniture loans, travel loans etc., and credit card balances as soon as possible! You'll be much better positioned to ensure that you can continue to use the magic 10% solution.

4. BE AN "OWNER" — NOT A "LOANER"

I can hear you now: "OK Coach," you're saying, "I'll start now; I'll invest regularly, saving 10% of my salary; I'll take advantage of the magic of compounding, and I'll make the Rule of 72 work for me. But tell me Coach, how do I get a 15% to 18% return on my money so that it doubles in four to five years?"

Achieving higher rates of return over the long term is simple. The trick is to be an owner, not a loaner.

But what are you really achieving? Despite the fact that many deposits in a bank or trust company are guaranteed at a fixed rate and by Canada Deposit Insurance Corporation against loss, you may still be losing — and losing something equally important —purchasing power.

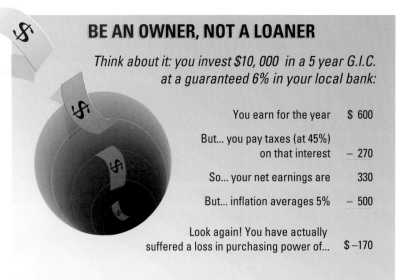

BE AN OWNER, NOT A LOANER

Think about it: you invest $10, 000 in a 5 year G.I.C. at a guaranteed 6% in your local bank:

You earn for the year	$ 600
But... you pay taxes (at 45%) on that interest	− 270
So... your net earnings are	330
But... inflation averages 5%	− 500
Look again! You have actually suffered a loss in purchasing power of...	$ −170

What you have been "guaranteed" by the bank is a loss of purchasing power because the guaranteed interest rate can't keep up with inflation and taxes!!

If it were consistently more advantageous for individuals and businesses to put their money in the bank than to invest in profit-seeking businesses, we would have a major problem. But that's not the case. In fact, just the opposite is true.

What's the difference? When you're a loaner, you lend money to the government (when you buy CSBs) or to the banks (if you put money there in term deposits or in Guaranteed Investment Certificates). You receive a guaranteed rate of return, have the knowledge that your money is secure, and sacrifice substantial growth potential.

Despite all our complaints and the constant focus in the media on problems, we're better off than ever before. Those of us lucky enough to live in Canada, which according to a new United Nations study is the best country in the world in which to reside, are better off than 90% of the world's population.

What's more, the next several decades will bring greater opportunities for growth than ever before in the history of mankind! The way to participate in all of this is to be an owner, not a loaner.

We know now that if you're a typical loaner, you're putting your money in the bank, or purchasing term deposits, GICs, or CSBs. But what's an owner?

An owner actually invests in the growth of the economy of this country or in the growth of the economy of other countries. While many people associate investment as an owner with investment in the stock market, this is not necessarily the case. It may involve ownership in mutual funds, real estate, or the stock market. The key is that traditionally, if your investment goes into ownership vehicles (stocks, mutual funds, real estate), your annual return may be 12% to 16% or even more. Take a look for example at the accompanying chart (TSE Trends, 1957-1993), showing the long-term growth of the stocks making up the Toronto Stock Exchange 300 Index.

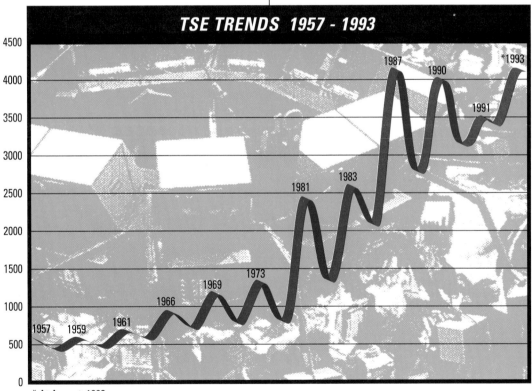

TSE TRENDS 1957 - 1993

* At August, 1993.

It's true there are no guarantees as an owner. The element of risk is always present in any investment that holds the potential of higher gains. You could earn no income or even lose part of your original investment, especially in the short term. But many ownership vehicles available have extremely good rates of return and long successful track records. And if you want to achieve growth to maximize your return, you must accept some risk. But history is on your side. So if you want to accumulate money to achieve growth — be an owner not a loaner!

Period from Dec. 31, 1967 to August 31, 1993.
Sources: Statistics Canada; Scotia McLeod; Toronto Stock Exchange; Bank of Canada Review; Mackenzie Financial Corporation.

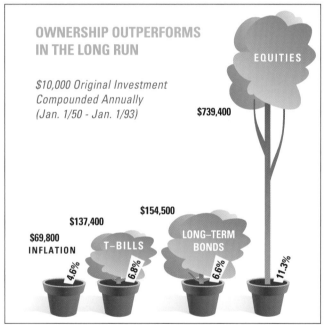

Sources: James Hatch and Robert White, *Canadian Stocks, Bonds, Bills and Inflation: 1950 – 1987;* updated with information supplied by Scotia McLeod.

The above chart, Ownership Outperforms in the Long Run, illustrates the compound annual return on investment of Treasury bills and bonds (loanership vehicles) over the past 43 years compared with the return achieved over the same period on the stock market (equities). You'll agree it's better to be an owner than a loaner.

This chart shows how a well-performing mutual fund like the Industrial Growth Fund has outperformed a variety of investments over the past 26 years.

To accumulate money to achieve growth, be an owner — not a loaner.

◆ ◆ ◆

5. PUT YOUR MONEY TO WORK IN MUTUAL FUNDS

WHAT IS A MUTUAL FUND?

A mutual fund is a "pool" of money to which thousands of people contribute. This pool of money is managed by professional money managers who invest the money in Treasury bills (T-bills), safe and secure government or corporate bonds, and in shares of generally proven Canadian and international corporations. They keep a watchful eye on the economy, on political, demographic and economic trends, and on international events in order to determine where and how the pool of money can be invested to produce the most solid long-term growth.

COACH'S QUOTE

"When you put your money in the bank, it goes to sleep. When you put your money in a mutual fund, it goes to work!"

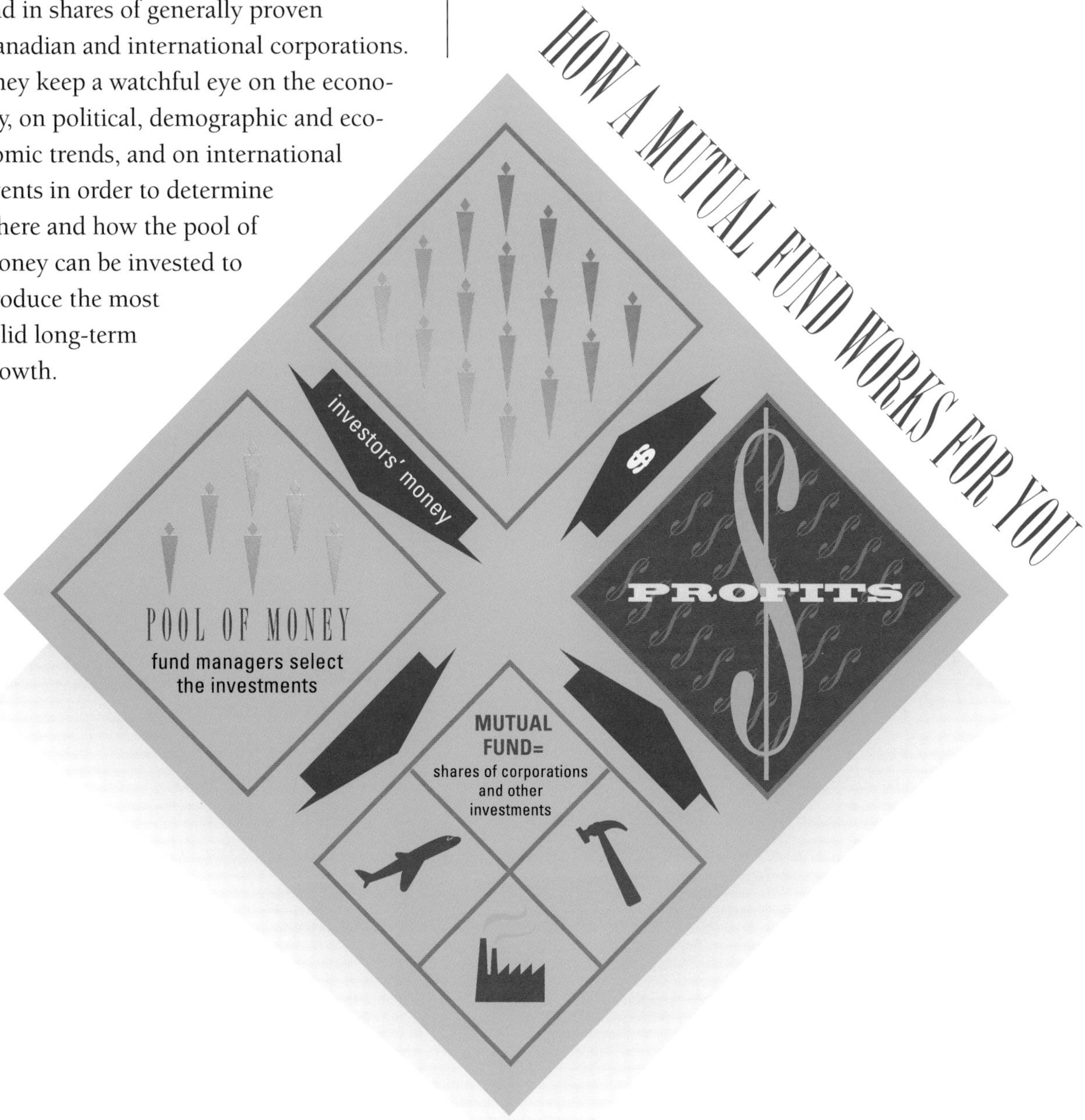

HOW A MUTUAL FUND WORKS FOR YOU

investors' money

POOL OF MONEY
fund managers select
the investments

PROFITS

MUTUAL
FUND=
shares of corporations
and other
investments

THE BENEFITS OF MUTUAL FUNDS

• *Professional money management*

Most people are too busy to take time to effectively oversee their financial affairs. They are also not trained to be expert money managers. By buying mutual funds, these people are receiving the benefit of the experience and skills of some of the best money managers in the world whose goal is to achieve long-term growth for the money they invest.

One of the most successful mutual funds ever, the Templeton Growth Fund, which is managed by Sir John Templeton and his management team, is a good example. Those who invested $10,000 in this fund when it began in 1954 saw their investment grow to be worth over $2.4 million by 1993. That's an average annual compounded growth rate of 15.3%!

Canada's Industrial Growth Fund was launched in 1967. A $10,000 investment in it then grew to $350,624 by June 1993. Its average annual compound rate of return to June 30, 1993 was 15.0% since inception and 14.3% over 20 years. These returns have earned Industrial Growth the honour of being Canada's top RRSP fund over 20 years. The fund is managed by the Mackenzie Financial Corporation, which manages more than $10 billion for over 650,000 investors.

• *Diversification*

Most people aren't wealthy enough to be able to diversify properly on their own by buying stocks of various companies in a number of countries. Because of the size of the mutual fund "pool," often totalling millions or billions of dollars, investors can purchase a share of a vast array of securities, bonds, and other investments. This allows you to achieve the peace of mind that comes from "not putting all your eggs in one basket."

• *"Hands-off" investment*

As mentioned earlier, most people don't have the time, the inclination, or the expertise to do the research necessary to make wise investment decisions. This is all looked after for investors by professional money managers for whom this is a full-time job.

• *Lots of choice*

Regardless of your circumstances, there are mutual funds that can meet your needs. Some people want income now; others, who will require income later, opt for growth now. Some investors are aggressive, while others are much more conservative. Some select equity funds, others prefer real estate funds, and still others like mortgage funds — or a mixture of each. Some wish to invest in specialty funds like gold; others like to invest in specific foreign regions like Japan or Europe. With several hundred funds available to select from, there is truly a fund to meet virtually every need.

In addition to these major benefits, there are other attractive features, too:

- Most funds allow initial purchases as low as $50 to $100.

- Most funds make it very easy to invest with a lump sum, pre-authorized chequing on a regular basis or through a group purchase with automatic payroll deduction.

- Mutual funds are "liquid" and can be sold easily and quickly; there is no minimum length of time required to hold the funds.

- Many funds are structured so that there is no acquisition fee and, depending on how long you hold the fund, there may be no exit fee either.

- A systematic withdrawal plan that meets your individual needs can be established as you near retirement and may require regular income.

It is important to note that mutual funds should be seen as long-term investments (i.e., they should be held for at least five years). Over this extended period of time, the economy and the market will most likely continue to develop and grow as will the value of your investments. For those willing and able to hold their shares over the long term,

there will be little need for concern. But for those who might consider purchasing for a hold of only a year or two, there is a greater degree of risk and the value of their funds might actually end up being lower than when they were purchased. For that reason, it's best to view a mutual fund as a long-term investment. When you do that, you have history on your side, for over the long term, mutual funds (which represent ownership) have significantly outperformed GICs (which represent loanership).

So be an owner, not a loaner!

One final note. In picking a mutual fund, look for a long successful track record and consistent management. Some funds do really well for a year or two and then "flame out" — often when a "star" manager leaves the fund's management team. Look for the ones with good rates of return over the long term (10 years plus).

For these reasons, mutual funds have come to be the investment of choice for growing numbers of Canadians who are trying to achieve exactly what you are: growth, tax relief, and security. In 1980, about $4.7 billion were invested in Canadian mutual funds. By June 1993, that figure had exploded to over $86 billion and is projected to skyrocket to $200 billion by the year 2000. Clearly, Canadians have discovered mutual funds.

TYPES OF MUTUAL FUNDS

1. Money Market Funds

Money Market Funds invest in short term money market instruments such as Treasury Bills whose maturities are less than one year. The objective is to provide a better return than savings accounts with minimal risk of capital. Money market instruments are very safe and have the highest available credit ratings among securities. These funds offer safety and liquidity.

2. Income or Mortgage Funds

These funds invest primarily in mortgages, as well as in other fixed income securities, such as bonds, and mortgage backed securities. The objective is to provide attractive income returns versus other fixed income securities (i.e. term deposits, GIC's etc.), with a high degree of safety.

3. Bond Funds

Bond funds primarily invest in government and corporate bonds and debentures, but many hold other fixed income securities. The objective is to provide income as well as safety afforded by government and corporate debt securities. Bond funds have moderate growth potential, especially when interest rates decline.

4. Balanced Funds

Balanced funds invest in a cross section of securities including bonds, debentures, preferred shares, common shares and cash. The objective is to provide a combination of safety (stability) through fixed income investments and dividend paying stocks and growth through common shares.

5. Dividend Funds

Dividend funds invest in a diversified portfolio of preferred shares and some common shares. Dividends from taxable Canadian corporations are subject to reduced taxes through the dividend tax credit. The objective is to provide attractive income returns on an after tax basis to investors. These funds also offer moderate growth potential.

6. Real Estate Funds

Real Estate funds invest in a diversified portfolio of real estate holdings. The objective is to provide attractive income as well as growth potential through the appreciation potential of the real estate holdings.

7. Equity Funds (also referred to as Common Stock Funds or Growth Funds)

Equity funds invest primarily in common shares of corporations. The equity funds available range from the very conservative blue chip funds to speculative or venture funds. Equity funds vary in the level of diversification and risk involved, but most funds have growth as their major investment objective. Some funds also generate dividend income. Historically returns on common shares have outperformed fixed income securities. However, on a year to year basis, common share returns can be volatile.

THE BEST WAY TO INVEST IN MUTUAL FUNDS

Ideally, every investor seeks to buy at a low price and sell at a higher price at a later date. The question is how to do that given the fact that there are market fluctuations. Nobody seems to mind the upward trends; it's those slides that upset us so much. However, by using a simple strategy called "dollar cost averaging," even the downside fluctuations can actually work to your advantage! It's as close as one can get to infallible investing — and most people don't even know about it.

Psychologically, if you are committed to regular investments and if you are prepared to invest over the long term, then downward trends (which are bound to come along) are simply opportunities to buy additional shares at lower than usual prices. As always, the upward trends will continue to be rewarding and satisfying.

Let's see how it actually works by using the following three examples. We're going to invest $100 a month for nine years (i.e., $10,800 will be invested).

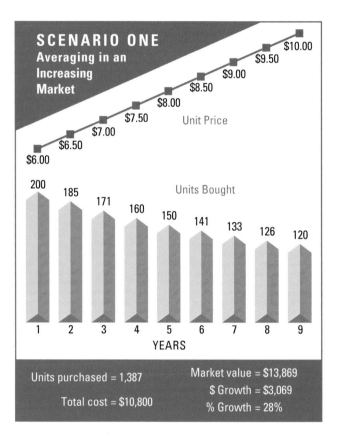

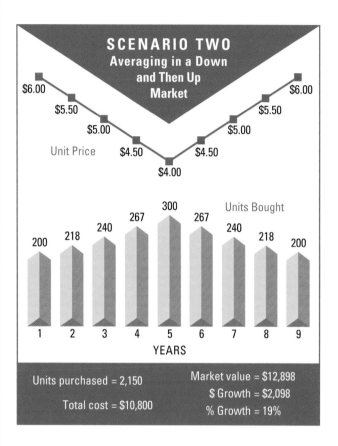

SCENARIO 1

Because the unit prices constantly increase, the number of units purchased each year actually declines as the chart shows. For example, in year one, the unit price is $6.00 and therefore $1,200 per year ($100 per month) buys 200 units. By the end of year six, the unit price has increased to $8.50, and therefore $1,200 buys only 141 units. At the end of nine years, when the unit price is $10, the value of the portfolio is $13,869 — a 28% increase.

SCENARIO 2

Notice here that for the first five years, the unit price declines. Imagine how happy you'd be in that situation! But patience is rewarded. The result of lower unit prices is that a larger number of units are purchased while you continue to invest $100 per month. Note that in Scenario 2 the original purchase price and the final purchase price are the same ($6). There is no market rise at all.

Despite this, 2,150 units have been acquired in this scenario. And even at a $6 unit price at the end of nine years, the value of the portfolio is $12,898 — a 19% increase. Significant growth in the value of your investment actually occurs in a declining and recovering market. You get the benefit of purchasing more mutual fund units when prices are at a reduced value.

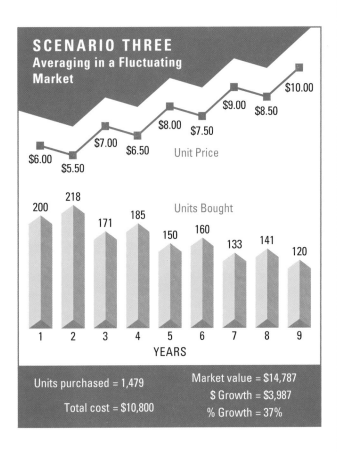

SCENARIO THREE
Averaging in a Fluctuating Market

$6.00 $5.50 $7.00 $6.50 $8.00 $7.50 $9.00 $8.50 $10.00

Unit Price

Units Bought

200   218   171   185   150   160   133   141   120

1   2   3   4   5   6   7   8   9
YEARS

Units purchased = 1,479
Total cost = $10,800

Market value = $14,787
$ Growth = $3,987
% Growth = 37%

SCENARIO 3

Here the unit price increases and decreases over time. Therefore, more units are purchased with the $1,200 in

some years than in others. This example is probably the most realistic in reflecting actual conditions. After nine years, the number of units purchased is greater than in Scenario 1 — 1,479 to be exact. At $10 per unit at the end of year nine, the investment is worth $14,787 — a 37% increase in value.

Thus you can see that the psychological barrier of purchasing more shares when prices are low (and that's the very best time to buy) is overcome by using dollar cost averaging. In fact, dollar cost averaging removes the problem of timing from investment management. By investing regularly, we don't get hung up on timing, for we've now got a logical comprehensive investment strategy based on confidence in the long-term health of the Canadian and international economies.

For most people, dollar cost averaging is the best way to invest.

Use dollar cost averaging as an effective system for buying mutual funds (or stocks) on a regular basis (usually monthly) with a fixed amount of money (usually $100 - $300).

COACH'S PLAYBOOK

The "Best" Time to Invest

How can you predict the "BEST" vs. the "WORST" time to invest? In some cases it just may not matter!

The illustrations below cover the last 24 years and the "BEST/WORST" days on which to have invested twenty-four different $5,000 net investments totalling $120,000. The results in each case can be helpful in deciding when to invest.

These are the results of having invested $5,000 in Templeton Growth Fund, Ltd. for each of the past 24 years on the day the Dow Jones Industrial Average reached its highest point of the year—the <u>peak for stock prices</u> each year.

These are the results of having invested $5,000 in Templeton Growth Fund, Ltd. for each of the past 24 years on the day the Dow Jones Industrial Average reached its lowest point of the year—the <u>bottom for stock prices</u> each year.

Date of Market High	Cumulative Investment	Value of Account on December 31	Date of Market Low	Cumulative Investment	Value of Account on December 31
5/14/69	$5,000	$5,449	12/17/69	$5,000	$5,210
12/29/70	10,000	9,822	5/26/70	10,000	9,666
4/28/71	15,000	17,166	11/23/71	15,000	17,277
12/11/72	20,000	33,815	1/26/72	20,000	36,731
1/11/73	25,000	34,945	12/03/73	25,000	37,975
3/13/74	30,000	34,685	12/06/74	30,000	38,314
7/15/75	35,000	53,843	1/02/75	35,000	61,121
9/21/76	40,000	83,682	1/02/76	40,000	95,604
1/03/77	45,000	116,345	11/02/77	45,000	130,921
9/08/78	50,000	155,014	2/28/78	50,000	175,659
10/05/79	55,000	198,155	11/07/79	55,000	224,510
11/20/80	60,000	260,272	4/21/80	60,000	296,285
4/27/81	65,000	262,518	9/25/81	65,000	298,979
12/27/82	70,000	306,504	8/12/82	70,000	350,083
11/29/83	75,000	417,274	1/03/83	75,000	477,664
1/06/84	80,000	458,454	7/24/84	80,000	524,402
12/16/85	85,000	624,516	1/04/85	85,000	715,430
12/02/86	90,000	752,618	1/22/86	90,000	862,614
8/25/87	95,000	718,303	10/19/87	95,000	823,525
10/21/88	100,000	811,729	1/20/88	100,000	930,667
10/09/89	105,000	987,907	1/03/89	105,000	1,133,111
7/16/90	110,000	857,875	10/11/90	110,000	984,492
12/31/91	115,000	1,123,116	1/09/91	115,000	1,289,918
6/01/92	120,000	1,298,295	10/09/92	120,000	1,490,691
Average annual rate of return: 17.3%			**Average annual rate of return: 18.2%**		

Source: Templeton Management Limited

Most investors would find the results in each case quite acceptable. As a result, it appears that—The "Best" Time to Invest is Whenever You Have The Money!

These illustrations represent the results of net investments. The rate of return and market value of an investment in the Fund will fluctuate, so that shares redeemed may be worth more or less than their original cost. The market is represented by the Dow Jones Industrial Average of 30 Stocks.

WHAT KIND OF FUND IS RIGHT FOR YOU?

LET'S START WITH YOUR AGE

No two people have the same investment needs. But there's a good chance that you'll have many of the same needs as people within your age group. So let's start there.

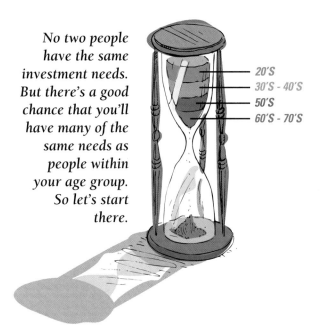

20'S
30'S - 40'S
50'S
60'S - 70'S

Perhaps you're just completing your education, establishing a home of your own, or starting a family. Either way, you'll have plenty of bills. And you'll need a savings plan to meet these obligations. But if you do have any excess cash, think about putting it into an RRSP or other investment that offers long-term growth potential.

With fewer debts and more assets, you're starting to make some progress. This is the time to be looking at growth oriented "ownership" investments. Why? Because historically, they have offered superior growth rates over the long term.

Your earnings are probably at (or near) their peak. And with the mortgage paid off (as it should be by now), you have more of that income available for investment. Growth is still important, but with retirement in sight, you'll need to start thinking of balancing your fund portfolio with income-producing investments.

Now you're ready to enjoy the rewards of a lifetime's work. Your investment needs will shift more to security and income. But you will still require some growth investments to provide a necessary hedge against inflation.

WEIGH YOUR NEEDS FOR SECURITY, INCOME, AND GROWTH

Considerations based on age, your personal need for security, income, and growth—as well as your tolerance for risk—will also influence your choice of mutual fund. After all, it's not worth investing in a top-performing growth fund if you're going to lie awake at night worrying that it might decline in value.

Basically, it all comes down to understanding yourself, and picking the type of fund that meets your personal needs. To assist in this process, consider the following statements. If you agree with a statement, mark an "x" on the left side of the scale. If you don't agree, mark it on the right. If you're not sure, mark both sides.

Agree Disagree

- Growth is my key investment objective right now. Income is less important.

- I'm interested in getting some tax relief from my investments.

- I understand that growth opportunities sometimes involve short-term risk.

- Investing is a long-term proposition for me. What I buy today, I don't expect to sell tomorrow.

- I recognize that, historically, "ownership" investments have provided better long-term rates of return than "loanership" investments. I want to be an "owner."

If you agree with all or most of the above statements you tend to be aggressive in your investment outlook. Conversely if you disagree your tendencies are probably conservative.

BALANCING YOUR MUTUAL FUND OBJECTIVES

Conservative.
Although you'll probably want to maintain a core portfolio of term deposits and GICs, you may want to investigate the potentially higher returns offered by income-oriented investments such as Money Market Funds, Bond Funds, and Mortgage Funds.

Moderate.
Security and income are important to you, but not to the point of excluding the higher potential returns offered by some growth investments. In this case, you should consider Balanced Funds, Asset Allocation Funds, or your own combination of income and growth funds.

Aggressive.
You want growth, and you have the time available to achieve it. A little short-term risk doesn't bother you if it means higher potential returns over the long term. You also want more dividends and capital gains in order to improve your after-tax return on non-RRSP investments. To meet these requirements, consider Growth or Equity Funds, and Dividend Funds.

THE BALANCED PORTFOLIO

Increasingly, research studies (including Nobel Prize winning work in 1990) are confirming the wisdom of the old adage that says, "Don't put all your eggs in one basket."

Up to 80% of the growth of our investments comes from the prudent balance we can achieve by allocating our resources across the main asset categories. At the same time, such asset balancing can help reduce the risk inherent in all asset categories.

To maximize growth and minimize risk is surely every investor's dream! Here's how it's done.

A well balanced portfolio will, over time, contain some holdings in each of the following categories.

Cash	Canadian Equities
Bonds	International Equities
Gold	Real Estate
	Oil & Gas

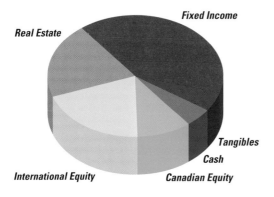

WHAT'S THE RIGHT BALANCE FOR ME?

The simple approach I recommend takes into account one's age and aggressiveness as an investor. A more aggressive investor might opt for a higher proportion of equities or stocks; a less aggressive investor may opt for more cash or fixed income assets.

Let's assume, as the table on page 39 does, that the investor is about 40 years of age and is moderately conservative. We therefore start with the age (40) and assemble a portfolio that has approximately 40% of its contents in fixed income or cash. An average 60 year old would have approximately 60% of her portfolio in fixed income and cash—and so on.

In our example, the client has 5% in cash and 35% in bonds—40% of the portfolio. Note, she also holds 10% in Canadian equities, 25% in international equities (because we need significant international representation), 20% in real estate (excluding the principal residence), 2.5% in oil and gas and 2.5% in gold. I usually recommend the oil and gas as well as the gold component be later additions to the portfolio.

Examine the table outlining the portfolio that has been developed for our 40 year old investor and note the major advantages of a balanced portfolio over the last 15 years:

1. The average return per year (13%) outperformed most other asset categories.

2. All asset categories except cash and the balanced portfolio showed negative returns in at least one year.

3. Except for cash, the range between the highest and lowest return in any category (i.e., the volatility) was lowest in the balanced portfolio.

4. The balanced portfolio outperformed cash on average, and is more favourably taxed than cash.

For many people, a properly balanced portfolio represents the means by which they can participate in the growth and favourable tax treatment of several asset types. At the same time, they enjoy the peace of mind that comes from having an investment which (in our example) has not declined in value during any one of the past fifteen years.

It seems that the caution to not put all your eggs in one basket makes not only "common sense" but also "research sense."

RETURNS BY ASSET TYPE

Asset Allocation	5%	35%	10%	25%	20%	2.50%	2.50%	100%
Year	Cash	Bonds	Canadian Equities	International Equities	Real Estate	Oil & Gas	Gold	Balanced Portfolio
1978	9	4	30	21	12	16	8	13
1979	12	-3	45	14	13	82	91	15
1980	13	7	30	33	23	46	43	21
1981	18	4	-10	-5	26	-29	-38	4
1982	14	35	6	21	1	-14	39	20
1983	9	12	36	25	7	19	-2	16
1984	11	15	-2	16	12	-19	-20	11
1985	10	21	25	40	10	11	33	24
1986	9	15	9	29	13	-2	29	17
1987	8	4	6	5	14	18	17	7
1988	9	10	11	10	17	-8	-28	10
1989	12	13	21	21	20	25	5	17
1990	13	8	-15	-12	5	-10	1	0
1991	9	22	12	22	0	-9	-12	14
1992	7	10	-1	6	-6	23	2	5
Average	11	12	13	16	11	10	11	13
Variation high to low	11	38	60	52	32	111	129	24
# of years of positive rates	15	14	11	13	14	8	10	15
# of years of negative rates	0	1	4	2	1	7	5	0

Courtesy of the Equion Group
Sources

Cash	91 day Canada T-bill
Bonds	Scotia McLeod Universe Bond Index prior to 1985 - Scotia McLeod Long Bond Index
Cdn. Equities	TSE 300 Return Index
Int'l Equities	50% Morgan Stanley World Total Return Index, 50% S&P 500
Real Estate	Russell Property Index prior to 1990 - Morguard Property Index
Oil & Gas	AGF Canadian Resource Fund
Gold	Gold Trust Mutual Fund

THE DOMINO EFFECT

As individuals, we often get so caught up in the details of economic developments that we lose sight of the "big picture." For example, we are informed several times a day of the price of gold, the value of the Canadian dollar, the current rate of inflation, the prime interest rate and the current level of the TSE and the Dow Jones Index. But we're not usually informed of the **significance** that these facts may hold for us, especially as they relate to the larger economic scene.

It may help therefore to step back a little and examine the four major asset categories—cash, bonds, equities and real estate—and see how they tend to behave at various stages of an economic cycle. By reviewing past experience, it may be possible to anticipate, at least in general terms, future developments.

Let's begin with cash. Late in an economic cycle, as the economy slows, inflation and interest rates tend to increase. As rates rise, cash, GICs, term deposits, and CSBs become more attractive to investors and, at this point in the cycle, cash is king! Remember 1981? Canada Saving Bonds paid 19.5% that year and other cash instruments were paying equally attractive rates.

But in 1982, Canada entered a period of recession and, as always during such a period, interest rates began to decline in order to stimulate economic recovery. Cash and cash equivalents lost their lustre and knowledgeable investors shifted to government and high-quality corporate bonds or to bond mutual funds. During periods of declining interest rates, bonds enjoy an increase in value (capital gain). During 1982 as interest rates declined, there was a strong bond rally with gains of as much as 35% during that one year period.

As interest rates reached lower levels in later 1982 and 1983, and the economy began to recover, the emphasis shifted again. This time it was away from bonds and towards stocks or equities. Over the next few years, from 1983 through 1987, the Dow Jones and the TSE reached new all time highs as the economy grew. During that period, the Dow Jones averaged about 26% per year!

As the overall economy continued to expand (even after the Crash of October 1987), business hired new staff, unemployment levels declined, public confidence grew and we began to experience the incredible real estate boom of the latter part of the '80's. It's been described as the greatest bull real estate market in history.

Over the course of that cycle, the emphasis moved from cash, to bonds, to equities and finally to real estate.

By the late 1980s and early in 1990, the cycle began to repeat itself. Inflation and interest rates rose and the economy began to cool. In 1989–90 interest rates reached 14.75% and cash was king again. We then headed into the recession of 1990–1992 and predictably, interests rates began to decline. Again, bonds come to the fore and had a strong run with increases of about 20% over that time.

As interest rates declined though, the shift moved again (if somewhat haltingly) to equities. In June of 1992, the Dow Jones broke 3,400 for the first time in history, although the rally was not sustained at that time. However, later in the year Canadian equities began to revive after several years of disappointing returns (i.e., during the time when cash and bonds were the stars). During the last quarter of 1992 and the first half of 1993, Canadian equities began to show significant growth suggesting that while there may still be some growth in bonds (as long-term rates continue to move gently lower), the impetus in this economic cycle had once again moved to equities. As evidence of this, the Dow Jones broke 3600 in August of 1993. Similarly, the TSE reached an all-time high during the same month. (See the table "A Nice Recovery for Canadian Equities on page 42.")

If the pattern holds, the economy will recover over a period of the next few years. Confidence will return to business people who see their business grow, and to consumers as job security, and unemployment figures begin to improve. At that point, real estate will likely return to favour and we will begin to see increased demand and rising prices. Whether we return to the heady real estate days of the late 1980s is debatable. But it does appear that as part of the trends described here, there will inevitably be growth in the real estate asset category.

In North America then, it appears we are experiencing the period in the economic cycle where the overall emphasis has moved from bonds to equities, and that we are still some time away from the move to real estate. On the other hand, Germany appears to be headed toward recession. Interest rates are high, but will probably decline as the government attempts to encourage economic recovery. For this reason, there appears to be investment opportunity in German bonds at the time of writing with their equities continuing to be some time away from recovery and growth.

For most people, the details of the price of gold or the value of the Canadian dollar presents little in the way of meaningful information. But an analysis of what's happening to the major asset categories—cash, bonds, equities and real estate—and an understanding of how the momentum appears to move from one to the other in a kind of "domino effect," can provide a more helpful and meaningful basis for investment decisions.

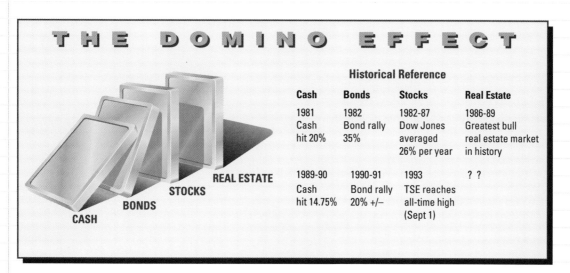

THE DOMINO EFFECT

Historical Reference

Cash	Bonds	Stocks	Real Estate
1981 Cash hit 20%	1982 Bond rally 35%	1982-87 Dow Jones averaged 26% per year	1986-89 Greatest bull real estate market in history
1989-90 Cash hit 14.75%	1990-91 Bond rally 20% +/–	1993 TSE reaches all-time high (Sept 1)	? ?

REAL ESTATE
STOCKS
BONDS
CASH

uage
ears.
rning
been
ional
bia.
years
sion
yle
orth
ritten
uver
tary
ince,
ram.
has
ment
ench
evers

based education, and has been highly involved in inservice development.

Secon
She ha
educat
Lorrai
guide
highl
develo
degre
of ele
experi
econd
Vanco
FSL-d
schoo
and s
includ
L for 1
been i

A NICE RECOVERY FOR CANADIAN EQUITIES!!

	3 month	6 month	12 month
AGF Growth Equity	19.8%	46.5%	59.1%
Altamira Resource	31.6%	74.1%	108.9%
Industrial Equity	25.0%	66.8%	91.9%
Industrial Growth	14.7%	35.2%	32.5%
Industrial Horizon	12.1%	26.5%	21.5%
Trimark Canadian	8.3%	21.0%	22.7%
Trimark Select Canada	7.2%	16.9%	17.5%
Universal Can Equity	15.1%	40.0%	34.9%
Universal Can Resource	35.4%	103.68%	177.19%

To June 30, 1993
Source: Globe & Mail Report on Mutual Funds

KEEP AN EYE ON INTEREST RATES

There is a multitude of economic indicators used to predict the direction of the economy. Everything from housing starts, to unemployment figures, to car sales and the price of gold is considered. For most of us, it's really very complicated.

Well here's a way to simplify the exercise by concentrating on one vital indicator: interest rates. It's not foolproof, but it can be very helpful.

Generally, high interest rates have a positive impact on savings, GICs, Treasury bills, mortgages (if you hold mortgages) and bonds. Conversely, high interest rates have a negative impact on businesses (borrowing costs are higher), stocks and real estate.

Low interest rates reverse the situation and exert a negative impact on savings,

GICs, Treasury bills, mortgages (if you are a mortgage holder) and bonds, while exerting a much more positive influence on businesses (which can expand more easily on borrowing costs that are lower), stocks and real estate.

Using this understanding of interest rates can help us to identify investment opportunities. Let's consider the current situation.

By historical standards, interest rates are quite low today: prime is at 5.75% (at the time of writing); five year GICs offer under 7%; CSBs pay 6.5%; T-bills are slightly above 6%; and savings accounts are under 2.0%!

In keeping with our understanding of interests rates, as they have declined recently, Canadian equities have been moving ahead nicely and Canadian equity mutual funds have averaged growth of over 27% over the last year (to June 30, 1993).

Similarly, we might also want to be considering investments in real estate. While real estate in some parts of the country continues to languish, it's quite likely that continued low interest rate levels will have a ripple effect—from enabling business expansion/creation to ultimately, recovery and growth in the real estate sector.

Clearly many factors impact upon an economic cycle and determine which asset categories will experience growth. But those who pay attention to interest rate movements can often anticipate areas of future opportunity.

INTEREST RATES: THE IMPACT ON ASSETS

Interest rate level

HIGH INTEREST RATES HAVE A POSITIVE IMPACT ON:
- Savings
- G.I.C.s
- T-Bills
- Mortgages
- Bonds

... AND A NEGATIVE IMPACT ON:
- Business
- Stocks
- Equities
- Real Estate

LOW INTEREST RATES HAVE A POSITIVE IMPACT ON:
- Business
- Stocks
- Equities
- Real Estate

... AND A NEGATIVE IMPACT ON:
- Savings
- G.I.C.s
- T-Bills
- Mortgages
- Bonds

CHOP TAXES

Sad to say, most Canadians pay more income tax than necessary — in many cases, a lot more!

As I said earlier, it's largely because they don't know the rules of the tax game, and they therefore play the game poorly. To make it even worse, many accountants (to whom we often look for assistance in this regard) see their job as to calculate the amount of tax we owe, rather than to educate their clients so they can plan wisely to reduce their tax burden.

We'll outline some of the best tax saving strategies for individuals a little later, but for now, look at this example.

Which would you prefer?

	A	B
Rate of return	16 %	16 %
Taxes (40%)	− 6.4 %	0 %
Inflation (5% average)	− 5 %	− 5 %
Real Rate of Return	= 4.6 %	= 11 %

Obviously you'd prefer a real rate of return of 11.0% rather than 4.6. Who wouldn't?

Notice that in our example, the only difference between A and B is in the amount of tax paid. How do you pay zero tax on an investment? Simple. Buy a Registered Retirement Savings Plan. As long as your money remains inside your RRSP, you pay no tax on it. It grows much more rapidly, and you're getting a much better real rate of return than you would otherwise.

COACH'S QUOTE

"Next to being shot at and missed, there's nothing quite as satisfying as a big tax refund."

Note that your investment goals of growth and tax relief are not mutually exclusive. Quite the opposite — they fit beautifully together in an RRSP.

EVERYBODY HAS A TAX PROBLEM

Earlier I pointed out how in 1993, 44% of the income of an average Canadian family was paid out in taxes of all sorts. I also showed how Tax Freedom Day, the day in the year when the average Canadian has paid all the taxes he or she owes to all levels of government, gets later each year.

You'll also remember that tax relief is one of the three key financial objectives for Canadians and that we should take advantage of tax breaks made available to us.

RETIREMENT REALITY

Retirement reality is often shockingly different from retirement dreaming or fantasizing. In the next few years, Canada will experience a dramatic increase in the number of seniors. As a result, there is no guarantee that social programs once considered universal will be continued. There is no contract with the government; programs can be wiped out. With so much doubt surrounding both employer pensions and public old age security programs, growing numbers of Canadians are concluding that their most reliable source of retirement will likely be their RRSPs.

It's clear then that saving for retirement is an absolute necessity for every Canadian and that we cannot rely on the government to take care of us in a way that will allow us to maintain our standard of living at the level we wish.

Over and over again, statistics show that many Canadians retire near or even below the poverty level. Hundreds of thousands of Canadians including professionals, sales people working on commission, owners of businesses, and employees of businesses — in fact nearly 60% of Canadians — do not belong to a pension plan. Nearly 50% of retired Canadians require some form of government assistance to survive!

Despite these scary facts, other statistics show in study after study that Canadians have the naive belief that somehow or other, the money they need in retirement will miraculously be there to allow them to live at the level to which they've become accustomed.

Remember, the reasonable goal for every Canadian should be to retire at the same income level as enjoyed in his or her peak earning years.

Let's say that Jack Cooper earns a salary of $50,000 in his final year at work. How much money would he need to have saved to achieve the goal of enjoying an income of $50,000 in retirement? If we assume a 10% return on his money, you can see that he would require a nest egg of $500,000 to achieve this goal ($500,000 x 10% = $50,000.) That's a lot of money!

Approximately 40% to 45% of Canadians contribute to pension plans, some of which are very good, providing 60% to 70% of the final year's salary. But even these people need to be putting aside money to make up that 30% to 40% shortfall.

Again, let's take the example of Jill Bowman who retires with a pension of 65% of her final year's salary; let's assume she was earning $60,000 in that final year. Her pension then would be about $40,000 and she'd need to ensure an extra income of $20,000 to achieve her goal. At a 10% return on her money, she would need about $200,000 in savings ($200,000 x 10% = $20,000).

Now some will say that in retirement, expenses are lower and that you don't need the same amount of income. I suppose there are some who go from work to retirement in a rocking chair, but I don't know many. My experience is that they're equally likely to be travelling, playing golf, or getting involved in a variety of sports or hobby activities — all of which cost money. Many people put off major trips until their retirement, when they'll have the time to go. But will they have the money? Don't accept the idea that you'll need less in retirement. It's not a necessary situation, but to avoid it you must plan ahead.

If all of this information about the amount of money required in retirement is depressing, let me now tell you the good news — and it is good news indeed. Not only will the government subsidize your RRSP contribution (in some cases over 50%) by allowing it as a deduction, it also allows the money to grow tax free as long as it's in the RRSP. Two fantastic advantages! And to make it even better, the government has recently raised RRSP contribution limits in a way that will be advantageous to thousands and thousands of Canadians.

RRSP Free Money Inside!

RCCH Revenue Canada Clearing House

Open this envelope immediately. It will change your life

Important details inside

TO: THE MONEY COACH

DON'T MISS YOUR CHANCE!!!

AN RRSP IS THE SOLUTION

Here are three key advantages of an RRSP.

Increased contribution limits

Starting in 1991, RRSP contribution limits for those who do not belong to a pension plan were increased to the lesser of 18% of earned income or $11,500. This figure is planned to increase by about $1,000 per year for several years.

RRSP CONTRIBUTION LIMITS

For those who do not contribute to a pension plan at work, the maximum RRSP contribution is 18% of earned income or the following, whichever is less:

1993	$12,500
1994	$13,500
1995	$14,500
1996	$15,500
1997	Indexed to inflation

Contribution limits are based on earned income for the previous year. Those who contribute to a pension plan at work are required to calculate a Pension Adjustment (P.A.). It's complicated, but fortunately the P.A. is indicated on your T4 slip.

Tax savings

The total amount contributed comes directly "off the top" of your income for tax purposes and can therefore significantly reduce the amount of income tax you pay each year.

For example, if you had earned income of $50,000 in 1993, you could con-tribute up to $9,000 in your RRSP (the lesser of $12,500 or 18% of earned income; 18% of $50,000 = $9,000). This means your earned income for tax purposes is $41,000. You would be approximately in the 42% tax bracket and would therefore get a tax saving in 1993 of about $3,780 (42% of $9,000). Now we're talking!

Tax-free growth

While the money you invest stays in the RRSP, it grows tax free. Using the Rule of 72, we can quickly calculate that at 12% it would double in only six years. Outside the RRSP and subject to tax at 42%, your investment would take over nine years to double.

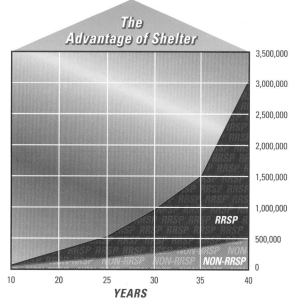

The Advantage of Shelter

Assumes annual contributions of $3,500 made at the beginning of the year; 12% average annual compound rate of return; 45% combined federal-provincial tax rate.

Start early!

Diane opens an RRSP at 12%, invests $2,000 per year for six years, and then stops. She makes no further contributions to the RRSP for the next 38 years.

Jim spends $2,000 per year for six years on himself, then opens an RRSP and contributes $2,000 per year at 12% for the next 38 years.

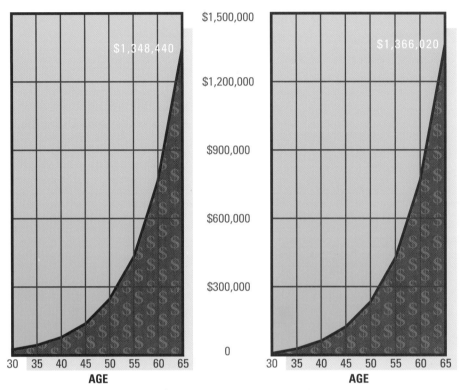

Assumes annual contributions of $2,000 made at the beginning of the year; 12% average annual compound rate of return.

See what happens! At age 65, Diane, who has invested only $12,000 has accumulated nearly as much as Jim, who has invested $76,000.

Start early and make the maximum RRSP contribution every year! Let time, compounding, and tax free growth in an RRSP work hard for you!

CONTRIBUTE MONTHLY

We've already encouraged you to use the Dollar Cost Averaging strategy, and examined the advantages of doing so. But there is another advantage in investing in your RRSP monthly rather than in a lump sum annually. For most people, it's just easier to find a smaller amount monthly than a larger amount annually...usually in February when you're still facing Christmas bills.

However, the major advantage is that you'll likely earn more by investing monthly. The following chart sums it up very succinctly.

Does $32,000 extra make it sound attractive? It should!

WHERE CAN YOU INVEST YOUR RRSP DOLLARS?

There is a wide range of options available for your RRSP. They include savings accounts, Canada Savings Bonds, Treasury bills, Canadian government and corporate bonds, Guaranteed Investment Certificates, term deposits, shares listed on certain Canadian stock exchanges, and a growing number of mutual funds that fulfill prescribed Canadian ownership limits. There are other possibilities as well, but these are the major ones.

In the past, the banks, trust companies, and life insurance companies have dominated the RRSP market, offering their "loanership" vehicles. Recently, however, as more and more people have come to learn the advantages and benefits of "ownership," mutual funds have become very popular as RRSP investments.

MONTHLY VS. ANNUAL CONTRIBUTIONS
(Using 12% Sample Rate)

$455,606	**$423,315**
$500 Monthly	$6,000 Annually

By contributing $500 monthly ($500 x 12 = $6,000) to an RRSP earning 12%, over 20 years, you would be left with $32,000 more than by contributing $6,000 annually at year end over the same period.

Money Coach Rule

I believe that for most people, a mutual fund selected to meet their investment objectives of growth, tax relief, and security should be the investment of choice because I believe that selected ownership will outperform loanership over the long term as it has in the past.

TAKE ADVANTAGE OF FOREIGN CONTENT RULES

Canada makes up only about 3% of the world's markets, so it makes good sense to diversify our investments and take advantage of the growth opportunities available in the other 97% of the world's markets.

In 1993 Revenue Canada rules allowed us to hold up to 18% of our RRSP in foreign content investments outside Canada. That limit is planned to increase to 20% in 1994.

The following is a great way to increase the foreign content of your RRSP beyond the stated limits. It's an approach that works best with a self-directed RRSP.

Begin by taking full advantage of the 18% allowed in 1993 and 20% allowed in 1994 for the foreign part of your ("direct") contributions.

Then, invest the non-foreign ("indirect") portion of your RRSP contribution in a mutual fund that qualifies as Canadian property but takes full advantage of the foreign content limits. The following example demonstrates how we can increase our foreign content component significantly.

Let's assume for simplicity, that you can contribute $10,000 to your RRSP in 1994. This means that $2,000 of the contribution (20%) can be invested in foreign holdings.

This leaves 8,000 to be invested in non-foreign investments. However, if you were to invest that $8,000 in a Canadian mutual fund which, in itself, has 20% of its holdings in foreign investments, it means that 20% of your $8,000 (i.e., $1,600) is also being invested outside the country. Therefore, you have increased your foreign investements to $3,600 ($2,000 + $1,600) or 36% of your 1994 contribution.

CONSIDER A SPOUSAL RRSP

A spousal RRSP is registered in the name of one spouse, but the contributions have come from the other spouse. These plans are particularly appropriate in a situation where one spouse may be at home and not earning much taxable income, and the other spouse is in a high tax bracket.

Let's say that Robert is earning a good salary and that his wife Michelle is at home raising a family. The strategy would be for Robert to contribute, let's say, $1,000 to an RRSP in Michelle's name — a spousal RRSP. Robert gets to claim the $1,000 deduction immediately, but when the funds are withdrawn in the future, they are taxed in Michelle's name. This is great for both of them since Robert, being in a higher tax bracket saves taxes now. Michelle, who will pay the tax on withdrawal, will likely be in a lower tax bracket and therefore pay less tax than Robert would if it were added to his already solid pension income.

SPOUSE AS BENEFICIARY

An important consideration if you are married is to name your spouse as beneficiary of your RRSP. If you do, the money can be transferred to your spouse's RRSP on your death and remain there tax free until he or she deregisters the plan. If you don't name your spouse as beneficiary, the RRSP will be included as income on your tax return in the year of your death and a substantial tax bill could result. Keep it in the family and don't let the government get any more taxes than necessary!

THE ULTIMATE RRSP STRATEGY: A GROUP PLAN

Recently, group RRSPs have started to become popular. Basically a group RRSP is a series of individual RRSPs held by people who all work for the same employer.

The main advantage of a group RRSP for the individual is that (in addition to all the other advantages of an RRSP) where monthly payroll deductions are made by the employer, the employee's taxes are automatically reduced. For example, a person in the 40% tax bracket contributing $300 per month in a group RRSP saves $120 per month in income tax and doesn't have to wait until income tax filing time to claim their deduction and get their rebate.

Of course, when we have a chance to get money from Revenue Canada now or later — get it now! For many people, this "forced saving" is the difference between contributing to the RRSP and

not doing so. Check to see if there's a group plan available where you work. If so, join it. If not, ask about setting one up. It's simple to do.

RRSP REPLAY

We've seen that many concepts I've been urging you to use thus far, are activated when you start an RRSP.

- Ideally you'll begin as soon as you start earning an income.

- You'll be an owner (through purchase of mutual funds) rather than a loaner.

- You'll use the Rule of 72 to calculate the time it'll take for your investment to double and always seek the highest rate of growth (that's consistent with reasonable security).

- You'll let the magic of compounding work for you.

- You'll invest a fixed amount monthly using dollar cost averaging.

- You'll get tax relief as a result of purchasing an RRSP.

Money Coach Rule

An early start on an RRSP is one of the best investments you can make, because it achieves all three investment goals: growth, tax relief, security.

OTHER STRATEGIES FOR SAVING INCOME TAX

I have commented throughout the book on the importance of taxes — particularly income tax. Taxes almost invariably get in the way of our achieving the return on our investments that we'd like. That's why it's important to be aware of opportunities available to legally reduce the amount of tax we pay. That process is called tax planning; it's the minimizing of the amount we pay in income tax through the proper handling of our financial affairs.

Tax planning involves using our knowledge of the rules, put in place by the government, to look for opportunities to reduce our taxable income. RRSPs are among the very best examples. Tax planning usually involves the assistance of a person whose judgement we trust, in whom we have confidence, and who is knowledgeable about the current tax rules...sounds like we're describing a money coach!

Tax planning is very different from tax evasion, which is illegal and which brings with it severe penalties including fines and possibly a jail term.

So, in addition to maximizing your RRSP contributions, how else can you save taxes? While there are tax saving opportunities available to individuals depending on their unique circumstances (e.g., business owners, the self employed, commissioned salespeople), the following are among the favourite and best tax savings strategies available to most Canadians today:

THE $100,000 LIFETIME CAPITAL GAIN EXEMPTION.

Currently in Canada there is provision for every individual to claim up to $100,000 in capital gains tax free during their lifetime. It's an opportunity that all serious investors should take advantage of fully.

A capital gain is achieved (in simplified terms) when an asset (such as units in a mutual fund, stocks, or bonds) is sold at a price higher then the original purchase price. For example, if you paid $50,000 for a stock portfolio and you subsequently sold it for $150,000, your capital gain would be $100,000. If you had not previously claimed any of your $100,000 exemption, then that $100,000 gain would be tax free.

It's true there are other calculations that ultimately determine the total amount of capital gain that can be claimed for tax purposes, but this example explains the concept. Ask your advisor to discuss this in more detail with you as it applies to your own situation.

Also bear in mind that the legislation in this area can continue to change. In the 1992 Federal Budget, amendments to the capital gains rules were introduced that would affect the capital gains exemption on certain types of real estate and on the tax treatment of a second residence such as a cottage or ski chalet.

Nonetheless, it's important to know of the existence of the capital gains rules in order that you can use them to your advantage.

INCOME SPLITTING.

This is a concept similar to the one contained in the spousal RRSP (see Page 50). Simply, it means that as much income as possible should be claimed by the lower-income earner. Interest from savings accounts should generally be claimed for tax purposes by the lower-income spouse — for example, a homemaker who may be without other income or with a small amount of income. That person must pay tax on the interest but will likely be in a lower tax bracket and will therefore pay less tax then the higher-income earner. The accompanying chart shows the significant effect of two spouses splitting income.

Over the years this kind of simple but effective strategy can save many, many dollars that are surely better in your hands than the hands of the friendly people at Revenue Canada!

SAVE TAXES THROUGH INCOME SPLITTING

The Usual Situation

	Jim	Peggy
Annual Retirement Income	$100,000	$0.00
Marginal Tax Rate	52.34%	0.00%
Tax Liability	$40,152	$0.00

The Income Splitting Strategy

	Jim	Peggy
Annual Retirement Income	$60,000	$40,000
Marginal Tax Rate	49.55%	41.86%
Tax Liability	$19,279	$10,635
Total Tax Liability		$29,914

Tax Savings: $10,238 after tax per year

CLAIM APPROPRIATE BUSINESS EXPENSES.

If you are operating a small personal business, most expenses that are paid out in the course of doing business or for the purpose of developing the business, can be used as deductions that may have the effect of reducing the amount of personal income tax you pay. This includes a salary that may be paid for work done by a spouse or child.

LIMITED PARTNERSHIP INVESTMENTS.

These investments, sometimes called "tax shelters," allow the investor to claim tax deductions, often of up to $20,000 per year, that can be applied to offset income from other sources — usually earned income.

Such investments have become so popular and are now so much a part of the mainstream of Canadian investment that they are now referred to specifically on our federal income tax return forms.

Such investments, even after the tax deductions are taken into account, often require an annual out-of-pocket, after-tax expense to the investor. It's important to note that these are investments first and tax shelters second. They should be seen as such and should not be purchased primarily because they save tax.

You will have to do your homework, ask probing questions, read the accompanying sales materials and legal documentation carefully, and ask for your advisor's opinion.

Limited partnerships come in many forms. In some cases, the limited partners invest in the production of movies or television series; in others they fund mining ventures for oil or gas.

Traditionally, the most popular limited partnerships are land-based, and range from the construction of residential townhouses or highrise apartments to commercial shopping plazas, or nursing homes. Limited partnerships that represent ownership in well located and fairly priced real estate still provide excellent opportunities for growth, for tax relief and for security.

Mutual fund limited partnership

More recently, the tremendous growth in mutual fund assets (over $86 billion as of June 30, 1993) has led to an innovative investment called a Mutual Fund Limited Partnership, which finances new fund sales.

The purpose of these investments is to pay the distribution costs on deferred sales charge (DSC) mutual funds.

Basically, investors become partners with the mutual fund companies and participate in the continuing growth of their funds. Significant tax advantages heighten the potential rewards and the on-going income helps offset the downside risk.

Remember your priorities

Don't lose sight of the priorities! Tax shelters should generally only be considered after you've paid off most or all of your mortgage, after you've made your annual RRSP contribution, after you've paid off virtually all outstanding loans, after you've got a growing 10% fund, and when you're earning substantial annual income. They're not for everybody, but at the right time and for the right person, they can be very attractive investments.

Keep up to date

These suggestions can be valuable as you try to take advantage of the income tax rules. But remember, the rules keep changing, and it's important to do your best to keep up with the changes that affect you. Large Canadian newspapers are giving increasing attention to business and financial matters, so I suggest you read papers like *The Financial Post, The Globe and Mail,* or the business section of your daily newspaper. In addition, a growing number of business magazines are available to help inform and entertain.

COACH'S QUOTE

"Paying less income tax is not the privilege of the rich; it's the plan of the wise"

BUILD YOUR DEFENCE

Security is definitely a vital investment objective and one which is taken seriously by virtually every investment manager.

Security is often achieved through "guarantees" offered by financial institutions which guarantee rates of interest to be paid to investors over various periods of time. The following instruments offer guarantees: term deposits, Guaranteed Investment Certificates, Canada Savings Bonds, mortgage-backed securities, and others.

Further security is offered to Canadians by the Canada Deposit Insurance Corporation (CDIC), which guarantees most deposits up to $60,000 against the default of the bank or trust company (but not credit union) that holds your funds.

But there is definitely a price to be paid for this security. For the most part, as described earlier, the price is a lower real rate of return paid by the bank or trust company. At best, you're treading water and it's probably fair to say that you'll never get rich by putting all your money in the bank.

As Canadians, we have traditionally craved security and guarantees. Every year we lend millions of dollars to the Government of Canada by buying what some people call Canada Sucker Bonds — CSBs. We deposit billions of dollars with banks, trust companies and insurance companies, and make them rich.

Of course security is important, and there is a place for "guaranteed" financial products in almost everyone's plan. But perhaps we should more often do what the banks and insurance companies do with our money once we've lent it to them at guaranteed, but comparatively low, rates of return. They invest it in mortgages and real estate, making higher rates of return, and keeping the difference for themselves.

In this section we'll take a look at how you can build your financial defence.

COACH'S PLAYBOOK

Establish an emergency fund

Many financial planners and advisers suggest that you establish an emergency fund equal to about three months' salary. For many people, that's an amount in the $10,000 range. But if this amount is sitting in a savings account, it's earning low rates of interest, and the interest earned is fully taxable. I believe it's far better to use the money to pay down your mortgage, pay off consumer debt, or "top up" your RRSP.

I believe that an emergency fund is worthwhile, but I feel that $5,000 should generally be the maximum amount you hold in cash. It's great to have a few thousand dollars available whenever you want it. You'll no doubt sleep better at night knowing you've got money in the bank, and knowing that you can act quickly if you see a really great bargain. But don't get carried away!

The alternative I recommend is that if you're concerned about needing cash quickly, you establish a line of credit in an amount from $3,000 to $10,000 or more with your local bank manager.

A line of credit for $3,000 means that you can write a cheque or cheques for up to that amount whenever you want even though you do not actually have the money in your account. You pay interest only on the amount actually used (e.g., you may write a cheque for $1,000 on a $3,000 line of credit; you pay interest only on the $1,000 amount). A line of credit, used effectively, can be a very valuable financial tool. Just be sure you pay it off as quickly as you can, particularly if you have used it for a consumer product, i.e., a car, stereo, trip, etc.

By establishing a line of credit, you can be sure money will be there if you need it and, at the same time, you'll be free to invest your assets in more productive ways.

HOME
Paid for
HOME

BE IT EVER SO HUMBLE, THERE'S NO PLACE LIKE HOME... ESPECIALLY IF IT'S PAID OFF

For many people, their home has been their very best investment. Depending on when they bought and what downpayment they had, they've probably made a solid return of between 10% and 15% average annual compound rate on their money. In dollar figures, most peoples' homes have increased substantially if not dramatically over the last 25 years.

For this and several other reasons, most Canadians seem to prefer home ownership.

• While it's true that there is some risk involved in the purchase of real estate, and while it's certainly not guaranteed that prices will steadily increase forever, I believe that if you choose a suitable location in an area with a diversified economy and hold your property over the long term, your home will increase in value. One recent study in Ontario confirmed that over a 30-year period, residential housing provided an average annual compound return of 11.95%. While no investments are "perfect," home ownership is probably in the "excellent" category.

• In addition to a probable 10% to 15% average annual compound rate of return, your principal residence is completely tax free on sale, which means that the real rate of return (average annual rate minus taxes…in this case zero…minus inflation) is likely to be somewhere around 5% to 10%, which is excellent.

You remember earlier I said that anything above a 3% real rate of return is outstanding. Because all the growth is tax free , some people accurately consider their home to be the ultimate tax shelter.

COACH'S QUOTE

"If you think nobody cares if you're alive, try missing a couple of mortgage payments."

• As well, the home symbolizes many of the true joys of life: children born and raised, happy holiday memories around a fireplace or by the pool. A home is far more than an investment; it's a way of life to the extent that many people don't even consider their home as anything other then a home. For most, even though they don't recognize it, it's far more than a place to live, and the phrase "joy of owning your own home" has more than one meaning.

• My grandfather used to say that the best way to save is to be forced to — through debt. Most people who buy a home today have some debt on it in the form of a mortgage. And most take their mortgage payments seriously (or they should). Thus a home can be seen as the ultimate in forced savings. Bit by bit the mortgage is paid off, and ultimately, we not only own the home outright, but are delighted to discover that it's worth far more than it was when we bought it!

HOME OWNERSHIP HAS REALLY PAID OFF!

According to a recent study by Clayton Research Associates, home ownership in Canada has proved to be an excellent investment over the 30 years from 1961 to 1991. The study sampled families who purchased homes at various times during the 30-year period — in St. John's, Halifax, Saint John, Charlottetown, Quebec City, Toronto, London, Winnipeg, Regina, Edmonton, and Victoria — and compared their average financial position with that of people who chose to pay rent and invest the equivalent of a down payment.

Here are some of the findings:

A significantly higher net worth among homeowners — $139,000 higher after 20 years, and $198,000 higher after 30 years.

In the future, home ownership will probably continue to be a good investment. Assuming inflation stays low at 2%, the Clayton study forecasts that homeowners will still be worth some $50,000 more than renters in 20 years, and $167,000 more after 30 years.

It's clear that there are many good reasons for purchasing if possible. But even if you do not purchase a home, it's not the end of the world! Certainly the place you live can be a centre of years of happy family activity whether it's rented or owned. And don't forget this ideal of home ownership is primarily a North American phenomenon. Millions and millions of people throughout the world rent rather than own their home or apartment and are content doing so.

But if we look at the owned home as a good investment, how can a renter achieve similar growth? Let's assume that Don can rent an apartment for $1,000 a month or buy it for $1,350 a month in mortgage costs — the difference is $350 per month. If Don rented all his life and invested the $350 (in addition to his 10% fund), he'd be in a very healthy financial condition. Remember the power of compounding over the long term? The difficulty might be that while he'd be forced to make the $1,350 payment monthly or lose the apartment, he might not be disciplined enough to set that extra $350 per month aside for 20 or 25 years.

PAY DOWN THE MORTGAGE FAST: HERE'S HOW

If you buy a home and have a mortgage, it probably represents your single biggest monthly commitment. It is also paid completely in after-tax dollars. ("After-tax dollars" means that every dollar paid off against your mortgage has already been taxed. So depending on your tax rate, you have to earn between $1.40 and $1.50 to pay off every dollar of your mortgage.) That's painful, and it's one reason to pay off your mortgage as quickly as you can.

The second reason you should pay off your mortgage fast is that it costs you a tremendous amount of interest when you have a mortgage. Did you know that if you pay off your mortgage over 25 years at 12%, it will cost you about double the amount you borrowed in interest plus the original amount you borrowed? Shocking but true!

The accompanying chart shows that at 12% over 25 years, it costs $251,520 to borrow $120,000! Fortunately, interest rates are lower now, but we still pay huge amounts of interest when we take a mortgage.

Money Coach Rule

Buy your own home if at all possible. The joy of home ownership, the tax free position on sale, the traditionally good rate of return on real estate, plus the fact that it's an excellent form of forced saving all make home ownership a very attractive goal for just about anyone.

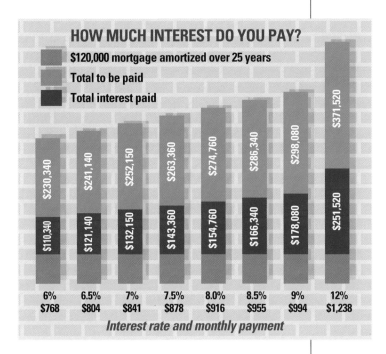

HOW MUCH INTEREST DO YOU PAY?

- $120,000 mortgage amortized over 25 years
- Total to be paid
- Total interest paid

$230,340	$241,140	$252,150	$263,360	$274,760	$286,340	$298,080	$371,520
$110,340	$121,140	$132,150	$143,360	$154,760	$166,340	$178,080	$251,520
6%	6.5%	7%	7.5%	8.0%	8.5%	9%	12%
$768	$804	$841	$878	$916	$955	$994	$1,238

Interest rate and monthly payment

These are two major reasons why you should pay off that mortgage as soon as possible.

What's the difference between mortgage term and amortization period?

As an introduction to this topic of mortgages, it's important to distinguish between a mortgage "term" and the "amortization period."

The mortgage term is the length of time the mortgage agreement is in effect. The mortgage agreement outlines (among other things) the interest rate, the frequency of payment, the amount to be paid each week or month, the penalty clauses if any, various paydown options and the length of the term (usually 6 months, 1 year, 2 years, 3 years, or 5 years).

The amortization period is the length of time it will take the mortgage to be completely paid off. The shorter the amortization period, the sooner the mortgage will be paid off.

Let's say you borrow $50,000 to buy a home (i.e., you take a $50,000 mortgage), taking a term of five years at 8.25% with a 25-year amortization.

It would cost $390.00 per month for five years. At the end of that time, if interest rates remained the same and you continued to pay $390.00 per month, you would have 20 years left to pay off the debt. However, if interest rates had gone up, your payments would have to increase too.

It's vital to know though, using the example above, that at the end of the first five-year term, you must not renew at a 25-year amortization, or you'll never pay the mortgage off! It must be renewed, in this example, at a 20-year amortization. Again, the shorter the period of amortization, the quicker the mortgage will be paid off.

COACH'S PLAYBOOK

Four great ways to pay off your mortgage fast

Now, let's look at four ways to pay off your mortgage as quickly as possible.

1. Reduce amortization period

Let's go back to the example we used earlier: A $50,000 mortgage at 8.25% costs $390.00 per month and amortized (paid off) in 25 years. Examine the chart on the left and note that over the 25-year life of the mortgage, the homeowner/borrower will pay a total of $116,884. Of that, $50,000 is the repayment of the principal, the rest is interest paid in after-tax dollars.

Now look at what happens if the borrower decides to take a 20-year amortization period. The monthly payments will increase by about only $30, but the debt will be paid off five years earlier, and he would have paid back $101,208 — a saving of over $15,000! If we really push to reduce the amortization period to 15 years, we pay $481 per month, or a total of $86,590 and save over $30,000 compared with the cost of a 25-year amortization.

When shopping for a mortgage, then, pay as much as you can afford monthly in order to obtain the shortest amortization period possible. You'll save thousands of dollars.

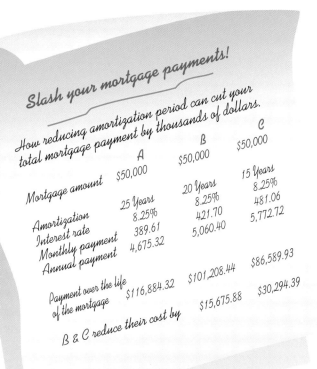

Slash your mortgage payments!

How reducing amortization period can cut your total mortgage payment by thousands of dollars.

	A	B	C
Mortgage amount	$50,000	$50,000	$50,000
Amortization	25 Years	20 Years	15 Years
Interest rate	8.25%	8.25%	8.25%
Monthly payment	389.61	421.70	481.06
Annual payment	4,675.32	5,060.40	5,772.72
Payment over the life of the mortgage	$116,884.32	$101,208.44	$86,589.93
B & C reduce their cost by		$15,675.88	$30,294.39

Save on mortgage interest!

How "doubling up" mortgage payments twice a year can cut mortgage interest by 36%!

	Regular Mortgage (25 years @8.25%)	2 Double-up payments per year
Mortgage principal	$90,000	$90,000
interest paid	$120,392	$77,140
interest saved		$43,252 (36%)
Years until mortgage paid off	25 years	17 years, 1 month

2. Make "double up payments" whenever possible

The chart on the right shows the value of making two "extra" monthly payments a year, i.e., making 14 payments a year rather than 12 .

Notice that the amount of interest saved by doing so is over $43,000. The result is that the mortgage will be paid off almost 8 years earlier than would otherwise have been the case. In effect, the amortization period has been reduced, and thousands of dollars have been saved because the "double up payments" serve to reduce the principal owing and therefore reduce the interest paid too.

3. Make weekly rather than monthly payments

The advantage here is similar to making double-up payments. By paying monthly, there are 12 cycles in the year. But by paying weekly , there are 13 cycles (i.e., 52 weeks/4 = 13 cycles). This extra "cycle" really constitutes a "double up payment" and has the effect of reducing the amortization period and therefore the amount of money actually paid.

4. Make lump sum payments

Many banks or trust companies that offer mortgages now allow the option of making a one time annual lump sum payment of 10% or even 15% of the original mortgage amount. If you borrowed $50,000 originally, you would be allowed to pay $5,000 (10%) or $7,500 (15%) against the principal amount annually — often on the anniversary date of the mortgage.

Again the effect is to reduce the amortization period, reduce the total amount of interest you pay by thousands of dollars and thus free your capital for other investments or important family or personal projects.

RRSP OR MORTGAGE PAYDOWN?

People often ask me whether they should contribute to their RRSP or pay down their mortgage.

The answer is yes—to both questions. Here's how I suggest they do it.

Make your maximum annual RRSP contribution if at all possible. One reason, of course, is to get a tax break, but the other factor is time. The longer your money is invested tax free, the larger the amount it will become. Don't wait to start your RRSP until you've paid off your mortgage—start now!

Then, take the tax savings you get from your RRSP contribution and use it to pay down your mortgage. If you contribute $6000 to your RRSP and get a $2500 tax return, put that against your mortgage. The rule of thumb is that by every dollar you reduce your mortgage, you save between $3 and $4 in interest payments over the life of your mortgage.

If you use this strategy every year, you can effectively build your RRSP and signifi-

LIFE INSURANCE: BUY TERM AND INVEST THE DIFFERENCE

It's probably fair to say that most people should have life insurance coverage equal to about five to 10 times their salary. Canadians average about three to four times their salary. Part of the reason is that we continue to buy a more expensive type of insurance than is necessary, and can't afford the right amount of coverage. This is a major problem, because life insurance is one of the most important purchases a family makes. It's therefore critical to make the right decision.

WHAT'S THE PURPOSE OF LIFE INSURANCE?

Life insurance is not really "life insurance" at all! It's probably better to call it income replacement insurance or financial protection for dependents. If you were to die tomorrow, your life insurance should replace your income for your dependents. But there's more to it than that!

HOW MUCH DO I NEED?

The answer probably is "more than you thought!" There are several things that insurance should do for your heirs:

It should replace your income

We have a habit of living to the level of our income. If you earned $50,000 at the time of your death, you will ideally have provided the means by which your family could continue to enjoy a $50,000 income after your death. How do you do this?

The simple answer is to say that you require 10 times the level of your current income in life insurance to ensure this level, i.e.,$50,000 income x 10 = $500,000 life insurance invested at 10% = $50,000. Of course, many people have term insurance coverage at work of up to three to five times their salary, and this should be a factor in deciding how much additional coverage is required. The truth is that while a 10% return is not impossible, the proceeds from a life insurance policy would probably be placed in a very conservative investment such as a GIC. So an 8% return may be more realistic. This means you would need $625,000 in coverage to ensure a $50,000 income in perpetuity for your heirs.

COACH'S QUOTE

"Lack of money is the root of all evil." — Mark Twain

It should consider the surviving spouse's No. 1 enemy: inflation

An insurance policy that provides a $50,000 income in year #1 is great! But, several years later, that $50,000 is significantly reduced in terms of purchasing power. That may put tremendous pressure on a family, especially if it means that an untrained spouse is forced to return to the work force. Even then, it may not be enough to keep the family afloat.

It's true many people may be prepared to return to work after the death of a spouse. While this may reduce the amount of insurance required to replace income, a general rule of thumb is that one should consider life insurance coverage ranging between five and 10 times the current gross income!

Inflation's effect on reducing purchasing power is the flip side of the power of compounding on savings. It must be considered in determining how much insurance is required, and it may require the purchase of up to an additional $100,000 or more of life insurance.

It should pay off all debt

This includes your mortgage and any other debt you may have, including car loans, bank loans, etc. The last thing a grieving spouse needs at the time of death is to be burdened with debt of any kind. The implication here is that both spouses should be covered to a level that will pay off all debt.

It should cover future obligations

These obligations would probably include immediate funeral expenses up to $10,000, current day-care expenses (if applicable), and longer-term university or college expenses. While you probably expect (as I do) that the student should cover at least some expenses, a sum for assistance should be incorporated here.

THE THEORY OF DECREASING RESPONSIBILITY

One of the most common misunderstandings about life insurance is a belief that it is a permanent need of families. This is not true! Life insurance is a means of "buying time" until you get your financial house in order. You need more coverage when you're younger — less when you're older.

YOUR INSURANCE NEEDS	
Early in life you require more coverage...	**Later in life you require less coverage...**
1. Debts are many (eg. mortgage, car) 2. Children are young 3. Loss of income would cause family suffering	1. Few debts (eg. no mortgage) 2. Children are grown 3. Saving for retirement
Few assets **Many obligations**	**Many assets** **Few obligations**

When your responsibilities are greatest, i.e., when you're young and have children and a mortgage, your insurance needs are greatest . As you age, your payments and mortgage are reduced until you reach the point of owning your home outright. This is the time when your death protection needs (in the form of insurance) are reduced and you should instead focus on accumulating cash for your retirement years.

WHAT KIND OF INSURANCE SHOULD I BUY?

You should buy low-cost, no-frill term insurance rather than more expensive whole life insurance and invest the difference between the cost of the two in a promising investment program. Specifically, I recommend you be the owner of one or more mutual funds either inside or outside an RRSP.

WHAT'S TERM INSURANCE?

Term insurance is a simple low cost insurance that has only one provision: If you die, your heirs will receive a stipulated amount of money. Period. In a sense, it's similar to home or car insurance. You want protection to a certain level for a certain period, as cheaply as you can get it! You'd laugh if someone suggested a savings or investment program should be part of your car or home insurance coverage.

WHAT'S WHOLE LIFE INSURANCE?

Whole life insurance offers a promise to pay a fixed amount (face value) on death combined with an investment or savings or "cash value" program that often pays a ridiculous 3% to 5%! But when you die, your beneficiary receives only the face value; the cash value stays with the insurance company. Can you believe it? This combination of features is called the "bundling concept."

CHOICE #1: WHOLE LIFE INSURANCE "THE BUNDLING CONCEPT"

Bundling is the major flaw of whole life insurance. With this type of policy, you are required to buy your death benefit protection and your cash value benefit in one policy. By bundling your protection and your cash accumulation, you get minimum coverage on death (only $200,000) and inadequate cash for retirement if you live.

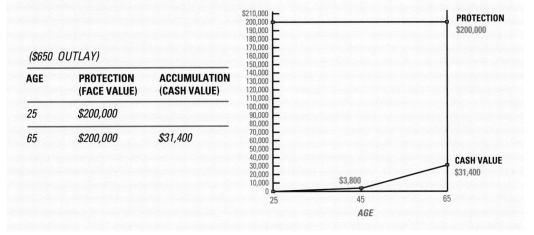

($650 OUTLAY)

AGE	PROTECTION (FACE VALUE)	ACCUMULATION (CASH VALUE)
25	$200,000	
65	$200,000	$31,400

Now let me suggest a much better option: Choice #2. Buy term and invest the difference in an RRSP!

CHOICE #2: BUY THE RIGHT KIND OF LIFE INSURANCE

Buy term (age 25)

WHOLE LIFE
(Guaranteed level Premium / non-participating)
$200,000 coverage
Annual Premium $650

TERM
(Guaranteed level Premium to 100)
$200,000 coverage
Annual Premium $450

- - -And invest the difference

Cash value after 20 years
(age 45) = **$3,800**
Cash value after 40 years
(age 65) = **$31,400**

Annual difference in premiums = $200

	INVESTED FOR	
	20 years (age 45)	40 years (age 65)
at 5%	**$6,943**	**$25,368**
at 6%	**$7,798**	**$32,809**
at 10%	**$12,600**	**$97,370**
at 12%	**$16,139**	**$171,830**
at 15%	**$23,562**	**$409,190**

Which would you prefer?

Note: Rates for choices 1 & 2 are based on 1993 rates of a leading Canadian insurance company. Rates and benefits vary by company.

INSURANCE REPLAY

Follow these rules/coaching tips for buying life insurance:

* Buy only low-cost term insurance. Compare the rates of several companies who offer term insurance and buy the least expensive policy you can find.

* Buy adequate coverage. While circumstances are different for everyone, a general rule of thumb is to hold coverage of between five and 10 times your current income.

* Compare the cost of term and whole life coverage — buy term and invest the difference. Be an owner and not a loaner, i.e., buy mutual funds — don't lend your money to a bank/trust company.

* Arrange for your coverage to decline as your assets increase over time.

* Singles and children generally require only enough insurance to cover burial costs. Singles who don't have dependents don't require income replacement.

*Children generally don't require anything more than burial expenses.

* Stay away from fancy and costly insurance options. Don't "load up" with accidental death, option to purchase additional insurance, child riders, etc.

* Mortgage insurance is nothing more than life insurance. Don't have a separate mortgage insurance policy; rather, increase the level of life coverage on both spouses. The same is true of short-term debt, i.e., bank and car loans, etc. It tends to be much more expensive to insure these loans than to buy additional life insurance.

SORRY STATISTICS

Still have to be convinced of the need to build your defence? Then consider the following facts from a StatsCan survey released in mid-1992:

* More than 4 out of every 10 Canadians in the years approaching retirement made no preparations for life after work.

* 48% of women age 65 to 69 in Canada live on less than $10,000 per year, which puts them at a poverty level.

* 18% of men age 65 to 69 in Canada live on less than $10,000 per year.

* Nearly 50% of Canada's seniors qualify for the Guaranteed Income Supplement, which is paid only to those below the poverty line.

ENRICH YOUR RETIREMENT

Three sure-fire ways to achieve growth, tax relief, and security at retirement

Gone are the days when, at age 65 with the obligatory company watch in hand, the retiree finds his rocking chair, lights up the pipe, and withdraws from life.

Today's retiree is often younger, healthier, involved in a variety of sports or activities, and determined not to withdraw from life . Today's retiree also has plans to travel, perhaps extensively, and recognizes that his or her involvement and interests can be comparatively expensive.

They also recognize that they have one quarter to one third of their life ahead of them. In many cases, particularly if they have a solid pension, today's retirees will be in the same tax bracket as they were when they were earning a salary! For all those reasons, while security will be a higher priority than it was earlier, one cannot ignore the other objectives of growth and tax relief! You can't finance one quarter to one third of your life if inflation is devouring your purchasing power.

1. ROLL YOUR RETIREMENT GRATUITY/RETIRING ALLOWANCE INTO AN RRSP

Many people receive a lump sum payment called a "retirement gratuity" or "retiring allowance" at the time of retirement. This amount is eligible to be "rolled over" into

an RRSP and under most circumstances should be.

If you do place it in a RRSP, you do not pay tax on it (which would be up to nearly 50% of the payment!), and it can continue to grow and compound tax free until you take it out. As we'll see in a moment, it can remain in your RRSP until you are 71.

Let's say you retire at 59, that you receive a retiring allowance of $40,000, and that you invest it and receive a 12% average annual return on the money. What will the $40,000 grow to by the time you turn 71? Well, the Rule of 72 tells us that at 12%, it would double in six years (72÷12 = 6). Therefore, it will grow to $80,000 when you're 65 (59 + 6), and to $160,000 by the time you turn 71 (65 + 6)!

You can be pretty conservative and still get 12%. Thus, by rolling over your retirement allowance into a conservative RRSP, you can still get growth (from $40,000 to $160,000), tax relief (you achieve tax-free growth within an RRSP), and security (through conservative investment).

2. Take advantage of the $6,000 spousal RRSP opportunity available

Through the end of 1994, it's possible to reduce your taxes, do some more income splitting, and receive some more tax-free growth by contributing up to $6,000 per year to your spouse's RRSP. As mentioned in an earlier section, you achieve several desirable goals by doing so.

You'll reduce your taxable income and therefore your tax bill.

You'll achieve tax free growth within your spouse's RRSP.

When the RRSP funds are drawn out by your spouse (and assuming that your spouse is in a lower tax bracket than you), he or she will pay fewer dollars in tax than you would have.

Again, by investing conservatively you'll be able to achieve all three investment objectives: growth, tax relief, and security.

3. LEAVE YOUR RRSPS IN PLACE AS LONG AS YOU CAN

It's important to leave your RRSPs as long as possible in order to allow the greatest amount of tax-free compounding that you can achieve and in order to defer paying taxes as long as possible. Current rules allow you to continue to hold RRSPs until the year in which you turn 71.

To do this of course, the corollary is that you will live on pension income or other earned income. You may wish to continue to work part time or on a consulting basis. These activities will generate earned income and, ideally, will allow you to leave your RRSPs undisturbed for the longest possible time, i.e., until 71.

If it is not possible to leave your RRSPs untouched until age 71, it's comforting to know that if you hold your RRSPs in mutual funds, you can easily arrange a periodic withdrawal program that meets your needs. Note that this is not generally true with GICs, which are "locked in" for a predetermined period of time, and it's another reason why I recommend the flexibility of mutual funds. It's important to remember that whenever you withdraw money from an RRSP, you pay tax on it, at your then-current marginal rate of tax.

A last quick word on inflation...it never retires! Historically, inflation has chewed away at our earning power at the rate of about 5% per year. Put another way, earnings must increase by at least 5% just to stay "even."

You may have just retired and have a current income of $40,000. You've likely got another 20 to 25 years to live. Look at the accompanying chart and note how much your annual income will have to be in 20 to 25 years just to keep up with inflation. I'll bet you're shocked at the figure!

Inflation at 5% Means Trouble				
PRESENT INCOME	10 YEARS	15 YEARS	20 YEARS	25 YEARS
$20,000	$32,578	$41,579	$53,066	$67,727
$25,000	$40,722	$51,973	$66,332	$84,659
$30,000	$48,867	$62,368	$79,599	$101,591
$35,000	$57,011	$72,762	$92,865	$118,522
$40,000	$65,156	$83,157	$106,132	$135,454
$45,000	$73,300	$93,552	$119,398	$152,386
$50,000	$81,445	$103,946	$132,665	$169,318
$55,000	$89,589	$114,341	$145,931	$186,250
$60,000	$97,734	$124,736	$159,198	$203,181

The chart above shows how much your income must grow just to meet the effects of 5% inflation. For example, today's $60,000 must grow to $203,181 in 25 years just to stay even with the higher cost of living brought on by inflation.

Remember too, you'll likely be paying tax on all your income.

Money Coach Rule

You simply cannot afford to ignore the importance of growth and tax relief as investment objectives even after you retire. If you do, it's at your peril!

HERE'S HOW TO ACHIEVE GROWTH, TAX RELIEF AND SECURITY AFTER AGE 71

Under current legislation, your RRSPs must be "collapsed" in the year in which you turn 71. What happens to your money then? Essentially you have five options:

1. Place your money in a Registered Retirement Income Fund (RRIF).

2. Buy a Life Income Fund (LIF).

3. Buy an annuity.

4. A combination of the three options outlined above.

5. Withdraw some or all of it and pay tax on it at that time. This option is not recommended unless income is required at that time.

In this section we'll examine the alternatives and offer suggestions.

WHAT IS A RRIF?

A RRIF is the logical extension of an RRSP because only RRSP funds can be transferred into it. Note the RRSP focuses on savings (registered retirement *savings* plan) and the RRIF emphasizes income (registered retirement *income* fund). You have been saving for several years, and now it's time to receive income.

A RRIF is structured such that a minimum annual withdrawal is required, although a larger withdrawal may be made.

The following chart shows minimum RRIF payments per year. Notice that while the former rules required a RRIF

MINIMUM RRIF PAYMENT

Age at the start of the year	1993 Rules %*
71	7.38
72	7.48
73	7.59
74	7.71
75	7.85
76	7.99
77	8.15
78	8.33
79	8.53
80	8.75
81	8.99
82	9.27
83	9.58
84	9.93
85	10.33
86	10.79
87	11.33
88	11.96
89	12.71
90	13.62
91	14.73
92	16.12
93	17.92
94	20.00
95	20.00
96	20.00
97	20.00
98	20.00
99	20.00
100	20.00

Source: Revenue Canada

* For ages less than 71, the original formula $\left(\dfrac{1}{90 - age}\right)$ will continue to apply.

balance of zero at age 90, a RRIF can now be held for life.

Note too that a RRIF can be purchased before age 71, but you must withdraw a minimum amount from a RRIF every year. Thus, because the withdrawn amount is taxed, it seems better under ideal conditions to delay purchase of a RRIF until it's necessary, i.e., age 71.

WHAT ARE THE ADVANTAGES OF A RRIF?

ADVANTAGE #1

All investments eligible for RRSPs are also eligible for RRIFs, so it's possible to continue to hold the same portfolio in your RRIF as you held in your RRSP if that's your wish. With a judicious mix of assets, it's still possible and indeed desirable to seek longer term growth within the RRIF, so that even though a minimum amount is withdrawn every year, the total income received may be dramatically greater than the original investment.

ADVANTAGE #2

RRIFs are designed to provide inflation protection through increased payments every year. You'll remember that we spoke earlier of the insidiousness of inflation and how it works to reduce our purchasing power continuously. Inflation will be with us throughout our lives, so the inflation protection provided by a RRIF is a real advantage.

HOW A RRIF FIGHTS INFLATION

Assume total RRIF value of $200,000

Minimum withdrawal

@ 71	$200,000 × 7.38% =	$14,760
@ 75	$200,000 × 7.85% =	$15,700
@ 85	$200,000 × 10.33% =	$20,660
@ 95	$200,000 × 20.00% =	$40,000

You can see from these figures how a RRIF ensures inflation protection by requiring an increased payout each year.

ADVANTAGE #3

Note that these are minimum withdrawals. Should you want or need a larger amount, that can easily be arranged. This flexibility is another RRIF advantage.

ADVANTAGE #4

The assets are yours! Estate planning is a part of retirement planning and it's important to know that if you die before age 90, any remaining RRIF assets go either to your spouse or your estate. Your spouse can continue to receive the annual payments if named beneficiary. If your beneficiary is not your spouse, taxes must be deducted from the fund balance before it's paid to the estate. Like an RRSP it's certainly preferable to make a spouse the beneficiary of your RRIF. In either event, the fact that you own a RRIF ensures that you can provide for your beneficiaries.

It's clear then that a RRIF has many advantages.

Money Coach Rule

RRIFs generally appear to do a better job of consistently achieving the goals of growth, tax relief, and security than an annuity. And that's why a RRIF is generally my choice.

WHAT IS A LIFE INCOME FUND (LIF)?

Until recently, retired Canadians who wanted to draw regular income from their locked-in pension money were required to buy an annuity soon after turning 71—there was no choice.

A LIF (which is now available in most provinces) represents an option whereby people with locked-in pensions can, if they wish, postpone buying an annuity until age 80 by purchasing a LIF.

One advantage of this new option is that a person is not forced to buy an annuity at age 71 when interest rates may be at unusually low levels. He or she can wait until interest rates rise and perhaps receive a higher level of income from the annuity, since annuity rates are closely connected to interest rates.

A second advantage is that, during the period between ages 71 and 80, the LIF can hold the same range of investments as a registered retirement income fund (RRIF) which may provide better growth, especially if interest rates are low during that particular period.

A third advantage is that if a person does select a guaranteed rate investment, it can be selected for a fixed period of time. At the end of that time the money is available for reinvestment (perhaps at a higher rate) for another period of time up to age 80. At that point an annuity must be purchased.

WHAT IS AN ANNUITY?

An annuity is simply a contract with an insurance company or other financial institution that promises you fixed, periodic payments for a set period in return for an initial lump-sum investment you make. When you buy an annuity you are essentially buying a stream of income.

Your investment decision is limited to the initial purchase, i.e., when to buy, what type to buy and from whom to buy. Beyond that initial decision, you have little flexibility to change your mind or the nature of your assets.

Annuities can be purchased from insurance and trust companies. Generally, your income is determined at the time of purchase, depending on the level of interest rates in the market at that time and you are usually "locked in" to that rate. This, of course, is attractive if you buy at a time when rates are higher than normal, and much less attractive if you buy when rates are uncharacteristically low. As a general rule of thumb, you can buy a monthly income stream that is approximately 1% of the funds used to buy it, i.e., a $100,000 annuity offers approximately $1,000 per month.

BASIC TYPES OF ANNUITY

There are three basic types of annuity:

1. LIFE ANNUITY

A life annuity pays the highest annual income for life, but payments cease entirely upon your death. If there are any assets remaining at the time of your death, they are kept by the insurance or trust company. In theory, it's possible for one to purchase a $100,000 annuity, receive one $1,000 payment and then die. The remaining $99,000 would remain the property of the insurance or trust company. Under this plan there would be no provision for any of the money to go to one's spouse or family.

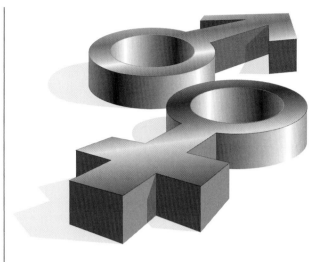

One way to avoid such an extreme situation is to purchase a life annuity with guaranteed term. The guaranteed term can be as short as five years or as long as the time until age 90.

Let's assume one purchased a plan like this with a 10-year guaranteed period and died in year six. The spouse or beneficiary would continue to receive payments for four more years. If at that time there are remaining assets, they remain the property of the insurance company or trust company. Note too that for every "extra" attached to this annuity, including the guaranteed period, the monthly income is reduced. (If you outlive the guaranteed period, you will continue to receive payments for the rest of your life — it is a life annuity.)

2. JOINT-AND-LAST-SURVIVOR LIFE ANNUITY

This type of annuity makes payments on the lives of two people, ensuring payments until the death of the last surviving spouse, and can be valuable in providing peace of mind that your spouse would be guaranteed a certain level of income even after your death.

This annuity can also be bought with a guaranteed term, and it is possible to arrange lower payments to the survivor after the death of a spouse. These can be 25% or 50% lower on the assumption that it costs less for one to live than two.

Again, the "extras" built into the plan will affect the monthly income received. In the situation described above, when the survivor accepts a lower payment on the death of a spouse, there would be slightly higher income when both were alive. But even here, the estate would receive nothing following the death of the last surviving spouse unless there was a guaranteed period attached to the annuity and it had not expired.

3. FIXED-TERM ANNUITY

This type provides payments for a fixed period of time — specifically until you or your spouse reach age 90. There are no further payments regardless of how long you live.

However, this annuity allows for your estate to receive any remaining payments after the death of both spouses if both deaths occur before age 90 — the end of the fixed term. The remaining money would be taxed as a total before being paid to the estate. In this respect, this annuity is different from the others mentioned above, which do not allow benefits to heirs; on the other hand, income ceases at age 90.

effectively meets the basic investment objectives of growth, tax relief, and security, it is true that for some people, certain aspects of an annuity may be particularly appealing. For example, for someone concerned about caring for a spouse until death regardless of age, a joint-and-last-survivor annuity may be appropriate.

These are critical decisions, and it's important to consult with your professional advisor who will be able to assist you in making the right decision and selecting the right option or options for you. Fortunately, it doesn't have to be either a RRIF or an annuity .

ANNUITIES IN SUMMARY

Overall, annuities tend to be less flexible than many people would like and certainly less flexible than a wisely selected RRIF.

When you purchase an annuity, you essentially turn your money over to an insurance or trust company, and you give up any future control over the funds. In return, you are promised an annual income. This income is usually fixed and therefore is eroded by inflation, although some annuities have now begun to introduce an inflation factor. When this is part of an annuity, a lower starting annual income almost invariably results.

A COMBINATION OF RRIFS AND ANNUITIES

Review the accompanying table, and select the options best suited to meet your needs. While I believe a RRIF most

RETIREMENT INCOME OPTIONS

Here are the retirement options that provide growth, tax relief, security.

| | ANNUITIES | | | RRSPs | RRIFs |
	LIFE ANNUITY	JOINT & LAST SURVIVOR	FIXED TERM		
GROWTH					
Growth potential	No	No	No	Yes	Yes
Compounding tax free	No	No	No	Yes	Yes
TAX RELIEF					
Minimizing taxes	Yes	Yes	Yes	Yes	Yes
SECURITY					
Payment flexibility	No*	No*	No*	Yes	Yes
Inflation protection	No*	No*	No*	Yes	Yes
Control over assets	No	No	No	Yes	Yes
Protection for spouse	No	Yes	Yes	Yes	Yes
Leaving an estate	No	No	Yes	Yes	Yes

*Some protection if you have indexed payments.

REVERSE MORTGAGE

Another option which is becoming increasingly popular with retired people is the reverse mortgage which allows people in retirement to use the equity which has been built up in their home over the years.

Here's how it works. A mortgage is taken out on the home. The owner has the option of taking up to about 35% of this mortgage money in cash, and the balance is used to buy an annuity. If a life annuity is selected, regular income will be received for life. If a joint and last survivor annuity is chosen, income will be received as long as one spouse remains alive. The income supplements any other source of retirement income which is being received.

When the owner or the last surviving spouse (if a joint annuity has been selected) dies, the house is sold and the principal as well as the interest which have been accruing over the years are repaid. Any remaining money goes to the estate.

On page 79 there is an example provided by Home Earnings Reverse Mortgage Corporation. In this case, the homeowner is age 74. The current value of the home is $250,000 and the mortgage available is $104,400 at an interest rate of 10.75% The owner has opted to take a lump sum payment of $4,400 with the remainder ($100,000) used to purchase a life annuity that generates monthly income of $993.79 as long as she lives (even though our examples run only to age 90).

Notice in the example that at 5% annual growth in the value of the home, if the owner remains in the program to age 90 or beyond, the mortgage amount becomes greater than the value of the home. In this case, the insurance company would suffer a loss, not the homeowner or her estate.

A reverse mortgage has many attractive features. All the income received is essentially tax free. No payments are made against the mortgage and the title to the home remains with the homeowner.

There are a couple of cautions however. For one, it's probably not wise to take a reverse mortgage at too early an age. One reason is that the younger you are, the longer you will be expected to live with the result that the annuity payments will be lower than you may wish or need. Another reason is that the longer your life expectancy, the more unpaid interest will accumulate on your mortgage and the size of the mortgage available to you will be reduced.

The second caution is that you may not be entirely comfortable with the fact that you are carrying a significant debt at an older age. Many of us work hard to be relieved of debt and a reverse mortgage puts us back in that position. As well, depending on the importance of leaving a substantial estate, a reverse mortgage may not be best for you since the mortgage and accumulated interest will be paid to the mortgage company and not to your heirs or estate.

But if you are comfortable with the debt while you're living and feel that the equity built up in your home over the years should be yours to enjoy, a reverse mortgage may be an ideal means of increasing your income level to one which will allow you to enjoy your retirement years more fully.

Age	Annual Income	Home Value Increasing at 5.00%			Home Value Increasing at 7.00%		
		Amount Owing	Home Value	Equity in Home	Amount Owing	Home Value	Equity in Home
74	11,925	104,400	250,000	145,600	104,400	250,000	145,600
75	11,925	115,925	262,500	146,575	115,925	267,500	151,575
76	11,925	128,721	275,625	146,904	128,721	286,225	157,504
77	11,925	142,931	289,406	146,475	142,931	306,261	163,330
78	11,925	158,709	303,877	145,168	158,709	327,699	168,990
79	11,925	176,229	319,070	142,842	176,229	350,638	174,409
80	11,925	195,682	335,024	139,342	195,682	375,183	179,500
81	11,925	217,283	351,775	134,492	217,283	401,445	184,162
82	11,925	241,269	369,364	128,095	241,269	429,547	188,277
83	11,925	267,903	387,832	119,929	267,903	459,615	191 712
84	11,925	297,476	407,224	109,747	297,476	491,788	194,312
85	11,925	330,314	427,585	97,271	330,314	526,213	195,899
86	11,925	366,777	448,964	82,187	366,777	563,048	196,270
87	11,925	407,266	471,412	64,147	407,266	602,461	195,196
88	11,925	452,223	494,983	42,760	452,223	644,634	192,410
89	11,925	502,144	519,732	17,588	502,144	689,758	187,614
90	11,925	557,575	545,719	0	557,575	738,041	180,466

Source: Home Earnings Reverse Mortgage Corporation

FINDING A MONEY COACH

I believe that, to a greater degree then ever before, it's important to take advantage of the expertise available from independent financial professionals.

* Accountants seem to automatically come to mind in this context, but I'm not sure they should. My experience has been that generally, CAs are far better at looking back and telling me what I've already done then they are at looking forward and telling me what I should do. And while they are often the best source of tax advice, they are not trained to look at the financial "big picture."

* Lawyers come to mind too, but their expertise is usually restricted to specific aspects of the law. And that's no assurance of either financial knowledge or the ability to make satisfactory financial recommendations.

My suggestion, therefore, is that you seek out a personal money coach who will take the time to get to know you, learn what you're trying to achieve, meet with you (and your spouse if applicable) in the comfort of your home, help you develop a simple but clear financial plan, and help you carry it out.

He or she should keep you informed (for example, through the publication of a regular newsletter) and meet with you at least annually to update and make "mid-course corrections" to your financial plan. It's an important relationship to develop and it can make a significant difference to your net worth, to your tax bill and to your retirement income.

COACH'S PLAYBOOK

How to choose your own money coach

If the services of a money coach are to be used to maximum advantage, it's important to select that coach wisely. Like any professional relationship, it will flourish if both parties remain comfortable in it, if there is trust and mutual respect, and if your confidence in the coach remains at a high level.

How then can you decide on who you will work with? The following guidelines can help.

1. Ask friends for referrals.

If a friend whose judgement and advice you trust can offer a referral based on their experience, you're probably going to be happy too.

2. Ask for the names of two or three current clients.

Call these people and ask them questions about their experience with this coach. Ask whether they would recommend him or her to their friends. Ask them what they like best about their coach, and finish by asking them what they like least about him or her. Their answer to that last question will tell you all you need to know.

3. Ask to see a few sample financial plans.

A reasonable plan should include information describing the current financial picture, an indication of desired future results that can be measured (complete with timelines), and a series of recommendations directly related to the desired future results. While many plans tend to go on for pages, I prefer them to be "one page simple."

4. Choose an independent

Some coaches are actually sales representatives for a single insurance company or group of mutual funds and can sell that insurance or those mutual funds only. Understandably, they will represent their product as being "all you'll ever need."

The fact is, however, that some mutual funds have performed better than others over the years and that some insurance companies offer lower rates than others. There are simply too many good products and companies out there to allow yourself to be restricted to the use of only one.

Work with an "independent" who represents a wide range of companies and products, and who will "shop the market" for you to offer the best products available. Within reason, I believe that a wider choice is better than a narrow choice.

5. Ask what range of services they provide.

The wider the range of services they provide, the easier it will be for you. Can they offer mutual funds, insurance, mortgage-backed securities, GICs, RRSPs, RRIFs, and annuities? Do they offer a mortgage-arranging service? Do they do income tax returns? Do they provide you with ongoing information updates through the use of a regular newsletter? Do they offer occasional large group presentations for their clients to be kept informed of changing tax law, economic conditions, etc?

Taken together, these guidelines can help you choose the coach who's right for you.

THE Winning ATTITUDE

If you wish to build financial freedom for you and your family, it's essential to begin the task as soon as possible. The principles I've outlined so far will put you on the right track. If you stick with them over the long term, you are virtually assured of outstanding success.

The sooner you apply them, the sooner and more effectively you'll be ensuring financial independence not only for yourself but also for future generations of your family!

Here's an example of how time and consistency along with the "magic" of compounding can ensure financial freedom for generations to come:

Let's assume you start with nothing — which is probably as true for you as it was for me.

You begin by saving $100 per month — more would be better, of course. In 20 years at a compound rate of 12%, you would have $91,121.

Now, let's say you wish to send your two children to university for a total of eight years, so you withdraw $10,000 per year ($5,000 every six months) for a total withdrawal of $80,000. Your original $91,121 minus the $80,000 would actually have grown to $91,714 (let's hear it for compounding!).

COACH'S QUOTE

"Whether you think you can do it or not, you're right." — Henry Ford

Now let's go even further and assume that you save $100 per month for 30 more years. Your $91,714 would grow to over $3,000,000!

Your children and their children of course continue to save $100 a month and for generations, your family will be able to use the investment that you started for education, housing, travel, emergencies, etc., and still pass it on to the next generations.

But as always, it's important to start now. As a friend of mine commented, "I should have started doing this stuff 20 years ago." I agreed. The best time to start was 20 years ago. The second best time to start is now!

Don't be discouraged by lost opportunities; focus on creating new opportunities for you, for your children, and for your children's children.

"I DON'T HAVE ANY MONEY"

Your altitude is determined by your attitude — attitude is everything!

There are books full of excuses for not acting: "The timing's not quite right." "I don't have any money." "I'm too busy right now." "I could never force myself to do that!"

All the education and knowledge available about how to become financially independent means absolutely nothing if you don't use that knowledge by applying it. It takes only a decision, commitment and a few dollars to start you on your way. Remember, it doesn't take a fortune to make a fortune; all it takes is some time.

But, the sad truth is that most people will not act because they simply don't believe it can work for them. They've conditioned themselves to accept being average and ordinary, to accept financial difficulty, to accept being poor and to accept being unhappy.

"THE TIMING'S NOT QUITE RIGHT"

Fortunately, as I speak in different cities, I'm seeing growing numbers of people who view themselves differently — they see themselves as winners. They think and act like winners, and they become winners. They're the people who can stay motivated and stick to their plan to achieve financial independence for as long as it takes to happen.

I'm noticing too that these often tend to be people who have their version of a money coach to work with and who helps them stay on course. Most definitely, there is a price to pay and priorities to be established and stuck to.

But I don't know anybody who has achieved financial independence who doesn't look back and say: "Yes, there was a price to pay but believe me, it was worth it!" Several of these people have told me too that if they had known how fantastic it would feel to be financially independent, they would have been willing to pay a much bigger price then they actually did.

"I'M TOO BUSY RIGHT NOW"

Remember, a winning, healthy, positive attitude is not with us at birth. It is not the result of an injection or a pill, it is not part of a university degree program, and it is definitely not for sale. It's much simpler than that! (I've said all along the great truths are the simplest!) It's the result of a simple decision that you have the ability to make. A decision to be extraordinary rather than ordinary, happy rather than sad, positive rather than negative, wealthy rather than poor — in short, a decision to be a winner in all areas of life.

Remember the goal? It's to create a situation whereby you retire at the same level of income as you enjoyed during your peak earning years. It's not going to happen by accident or by magic. It's going to happen because you make it happen through a simple but deliberate long term plan. It's going to happen over a period of time because you have not only learned what needs to be done — you have *done* what needs to be done.

POST-GAME RECAP

How to Achieve Financial Independence

1. Pay yourself first

2. Invest consistently and over the long term (time and consistency)

3. Maximize your RRSP contribution every year using dollar cost averaging

4. Become an owner, not a loaner

5. Invest in solidly performing, well managed mutual funds

6. Learn and apply the magic of compounding

7. Learn and use the rule of 72 to enable your money to double as quickly as possible

8. Pay off your mortgage

9. Buy low-cost term insurance only

10. Pay your credit cards off monthly

11. Use all the tax saving options at your disposal

Money Coach Rule

If you can dream it, you can do it! Do it right and do it now!

A GLOSSARY OF TERMS

Amortization: The process of gradually reducing a future obligation or capital outlay with a series of payments over a pre-determined period.

Annuity: An agreement under which assets are turned over to an institution on the condition that the donor (or other designated person) receive regular payments for a specified period. Most often used as a retirement vehicle to provide the annuitant with a guaranteed income. Life annuities pay for the lifetime of the annuitant and fixed-term annuities until the annuitant reaches age 90.

Asset allocation: The relative proportions of equities, bonds, cash, real estate and other asset types held in a portfolio at a given time. In a mutual fund, the portfolio manager often varies these proportions in order to maximize return when economic conditions change.

Automatic reinvestment: An option available to investors in mutual fund or other investment whereby income (dividends, interest, or capital gains) distributions paid are used to purchase additional units of the fund.

Balanced portfolio: A balanced portfolio is the distribution of investments into several asset categories to help increase returns and reduce risk. The basic components of a balanced portfolio are cash, bonds, Canadian and international equities, real estate, oil, gas and gold. The weighting of the different components varies depending on age and one's aggressiveness as an investor.

Bear market: A stock market whose index of representative stocks, such as the Toronto Stock Exchange 300 Composite Index, is declining in value. A "bearish" investor believes share prices will fall.

Blue chip stocks: Stocks with good investment qualities. They are usually common shares of well-established companies with good earning records and regular dividend payments that are known nationally for the quality and wide acceptance of their products and services.

Bond: A debt instrument issued by governments and corporations. A bond is a promise by the issuer to pay the full amount of the debt on maturity, plus interest payments at regular intervals.

Bull market: A stock market whose index has been rising in value. A "bullish" investor believes share prices will rise.

Canada Pension Plan (Quebec Pension Plan for residents of that province): Begun in 1966, CPP benefits are available to all working Canadians who have contributed to it. The amount of benefits paid depends on contributions made (most people will have paid the maximum) and your age.

Canada Deposit Insurance Corporation (CDIC): An agency of the Government of Canada which insures the deposits of Canadians in banks and trust companies up to $60,000.

Capital gain: A profit made on the sale of an asset when the market price rises above the purchase price — usually in real estate, stocks, bonds, or other capital assets.

Common share: A class of stock that represents ownership, or equity, in a company. Common shares entitle the holder to a share in the company's profits, usually as a dividend. They may also carry a voting privilege.

Compounding: Reinvesting interest as capital to earn additional interest.

Compound interest: Interest earned on the amount invested, plus previously accumulated interest earnings. This may occur daily, weekly, monthly, quarterly, semi-annually, or annually.

Convertible term: Term life insurance which can be converted to any permanent or whole life policy without evidence of insurability, subject to time limitations.

Decreasing term: Insurance benefits reduced monthly or yearly with the premium remaining constant. (In standard policies, premiums increase and benefits remain constant.)

Deferred annuity: An annuity where payments begin after the annuity is purchased — usually after a given number of years or at certain ages.

Deferred Sales Charge (DSC): An increasingly popular alternative for mutual funds that charge front-end acquisition fees. Here, a fee is paid when the investor sells units in the fund. This usually begins at 4.5% of the units' value in the first year and declines by 0.5% to 1% per year, eventually reaching 0% several years into the future. Sometimes called an Exit Fee.

Distributions: The payments made by a mutual fund to its unit holders of the interest, dividends, and/or capital gains earned during the year. Shareholders may either take distributions in cash or reinvest them in additional shares of the fund.

Diversification: Spreading investment risk by investing in a variety of companies operating in different industries and/or countries.

Dividend: A portion of a company's profit paid out to common and preferred shareholders, the amount having been decided on by the company's board of directors. A dividend may be in the form of cash or additional stock. A preferred dividend is usually a fixed amount, while a common dividend may fluctuate with the earnings of the company.

Dollar cost averaging: An investment program in which contributions are made at regular intervals with specific and equal dollar amounts. This often results in a lower average cost per unit because more units are purchased when the prices are depressed than when they are high.

Earned income: For tax purposes, loosely defined as the total of income from employment, self-employment, pensions and alimony. Losses from rental property and self employment may be deducted from these amounts.

Equity funds: Mutual funds that invest in common and preferred shares.

Estate: All assets owned by an individual at the time of death. The estate includes all funds, personal effects, interests in business enterprises, titles to property, real estate and chattels, and evidence of ownership, such as stocks, bonds, and mortgages owned, and notes receivable.

Exchange privilege: The ability of a shareholder to transfer investments from one mutual fund to another within a "family" of funds managed by the same company. This exchange may or may not be accompanied by a transaction fee which is based on the asset value of the transfer.

Ex-Dividend: The date on which distributions that have been declared by a mutual fund are deducted from total net assets. The price of the fund's shares or units will be reduced by the amount of the distribution.

Exit fee: See *Deferred Sales Charge*.

Fixed-income funds: Mutual funds that invest in mortgages, bonds, or a combination of both. Mortgages and bonds are issued at a fixed rate of interest and are known as fixed-income securities.

Front end commission charge: An acquisition fee based on the total value of mutual fund units purchased. The fees can range from 2% to 9%, but average 4% to 5% on most purchases.

GIC: Guaranteed investment certificate. A deposit certificate usually issued by a bank or trust company. An interest bearing investment that matures after a specified term, usually anywhere from 30 days to 5 years. The interest remains fixed during this period.

Growth stock: Shares of a company whose earnings are expected to grow faster than average.

Guaranteed Income Supplement: A monthly payment made by the federal government to low income households. It is based on a means test and paid only to seniors with little or no income beyond Old Age Security (OAS) payments.

Guaranteed term: The length of time for which annuity payments are guaranteed. If the annuitant dies before the specified term, payments to the beneficiary will continue until the term ends.

Income splitting: The process of diverting taxable income from an individual in a high tax bracket to one in a lower tax bracket.

Index fund: A mutual fund designed to match the performance of a recognized group of publicly traded stocks, such as those represented by the TSE 300 Index or the Standard & Poor's 500 Index in the US.

Interest: What a borrower is obliged to pay to a lender for the use of a fixed sum of money.

Intestate: The legal status of someone who dies without leaving a valid will.

Investment: Using money for the purpose of obtaining income, capital gains, or both.

Investment fund: See *Mutual fund*.

Joint and last survivor: A type of annuity that pays benefits until both annuitant and the annuitant's spouse die.

Leverage: Using borrowed funds to maximize the rate of return on investment. A potentially dangerous strategy if the investment declines in value.

LIF (Life Income Fund): An investment option now available to people who do not wish to use locked-in RRSP funds to buy an annuity at age 71. Purchase of a LIF allows one to delay the purchase of an annuity until age 80. A LIF is eligible to use the same range of investments available in a RRIF.

Limited partnership: See *Tax shelter*.

Line of credit: A flexible type of borrowing facility that allows you to borrow up to a prescribed limit and pay interest only on the amount used.

Liquidity: The ease with which an asset can be sold and converted into cash at its full value.

Management fee: The amount paid annually by a mutual fund to its managers. The average annual fee in Canada is between 1 and 2% of the value of the fund's assets.

Marginal tax rate: The rate at which tax is calculated on the next dollar of income earned. This rate increases at progressively higher income brackets.

Market timing: The process of shifting from one type of investment to another with the intention of maximizing your return as market conditions change.

MBS: Mortgage backed securities; they provide higher yields than many other savings options by investing in first mortgages on residential properties.

Money market fund: Fixed income mutual funds that invest in short-term securities (maturing within one year).

Mortgage: A legal instrument given by a borrower to the lender entitling the lender to take over pledged property if conditions of the loan are not met.

Mutual fund: A professionally managed pool of assets, representing the contributions of many investors, which is used to purchase a portfolio of securities that meets specific investment objectives. Units are offered for sale by the fund on a continuous basis; the fund will also buy back units at their current price (net asset value per share). Sometimes called an investment fund. The most common type of fund is known as an "open end fund."

Net Asset Value Per Share (NAVPS): The total market value of all securities owned by a mutual fund, less its liabilities, divided by the number of units outstanding.

No-load fund: A mutual fund that does not charge a fee for buying or selling its units.

Old Age Security: Federal government benefits paid monthly to all Canadians at age 65, whether or not they are retired. Payments are indexed to inflation.

Personal net worth: The difference between your assets and your liabilities.

Portfolio: A group of securities held or owned for investment purposes by an individual or institution. An investor's portfolio may contain common and preferred shares, bonds, options, and other types of securities.

Power of attorney: Gives signing authority for your affairs to a spouse or other trusted person in case of accident or other circumstances that leave you unable to manage your own affairs.

Prospectus: A legal document describing a new issue of securities or a mutual fund that is to be sold to the public. The prospectus must be prepared in accordance with provincial securities commission regulations. It must contain information on any material facts that can have an impact on the value of the investment—such as the fund's investment objectives and policies, services offered, or fees charged. It must also identify any investment restrictions, as well as the officers of the company.

Real rate of return: The stated rate of return, less inflation and taxes.

Renewable term: A term life insurance policy that may be renewed at prescribed rates without evidence of insurability.

RESP: Registered Education Savings Plan. A savings program for post–secondary education which earns tax-sheltered income. This income is taxable when taken out by the beneficiary of the plan, but he or she will usually have limited income when at school, and will therefore pay little tax.

Retirement gratuity: See *Retiring allowance*.

Retiring allowance: A lump sum paid to some employees on retirement. Usually the amount is limited to the equivalent of 50% of the final year's salary. Can be "rolled" into an RRSP.

Reverse mortgage: A means of borrowing that allows a retired homeowner to use the equity built up in a home to receive a lump sum of cash, as well as monthly tax-free income through the purchase of an annuity.

Risk: The possibility that some or all of the money put into an investment will be lost.

Risk-free return: The return available from securities that have no risk of loss. Short term securities issued by the government (such as Treasury bills) normally provide a risk-free return.

Risk tolerance: The ability of a person to tolerate risk. Risk tolerance is a function of the individual's personality and other factors, and is an important element in determining investment strategy.

RRIF: Registered Retirement Income Fund. A non-annuity investment vehicle for maturing RRSPs. One of the options available to RRSP holders upon cashing in their retirement funds at age 71 or sooner. RRIFs generally provide for a series of payments which increase each year.

RRSP: Registered Retirement Savings Plan. A savings program approved by Revenue Canada that permits tax-deferred saving for retirement purposes. Contributions to an RRSP are tax deductible. Earnings on contributions are sheltered from tax while they remain in the plan.

Rule of 72: A simple mathematical calculation used to determine how quickly money doubles in value. In order to determine the number of years required, divide 72 by the rate of return.

Self-directed RRSP: An RRSP whose investments are controlled by the plan holder. A self-directed RRSP may include stocks, bonds, residential mortgages, or other types of investments approved by Revenue Canada.

Spousal RRSP contribution: A contribution by a taxpayer to an RRSP held by his or her spouse. The amount is counted against the contributor's yearly RRSP limit and can be used as a tax deduction on the contributor's tax return, but remains part of the spouse's plan.

Tax deferral: The use of various (legal) methods to postpone the payment of income taxes until a later date.

Tax shelter: An investment that, by government regulation, can be made with untaxed or partly-taxed dollars. The creation of tax losses in order to offset an individual's taxable income from other sources thereby reduces tax liability.

Taxable income: The amount of your annual income that is used to calculate how much income tax must be paid; your total earnings for the year, minus deductions.

Term deposit: Similar to a guaranteed investment certificate. An interest-bearing investment to which an investor commits funds for a specified term and rate of interest.

Term insurance: A form of life insurance designed to provide coverage over a specific period.

Total return: The amount of income earned from an investment, together with its capital appreciation, expressed as a percentage of the original amount invested. It indicates an investment's performance over a stated period.

Treasury bills: Short-term debt securities sold by governments, usually with maturities of three months to one year. They carry no stated interest rate, but trade at a discount to their face value. The discount represents the return.

Unit: In mutual funds, a unit represents a portion, or share, of the total value of the fund. Units are purchased by investors, and rise or fall proportionately with the net asset value of the fund.

Whole life: Life insurance policies that provide a death benefit and cash value. The cash value is funded by premiums that are much higher than the actual cost of the coverage—particularly in the early years of the policy.